sister *of* darkness

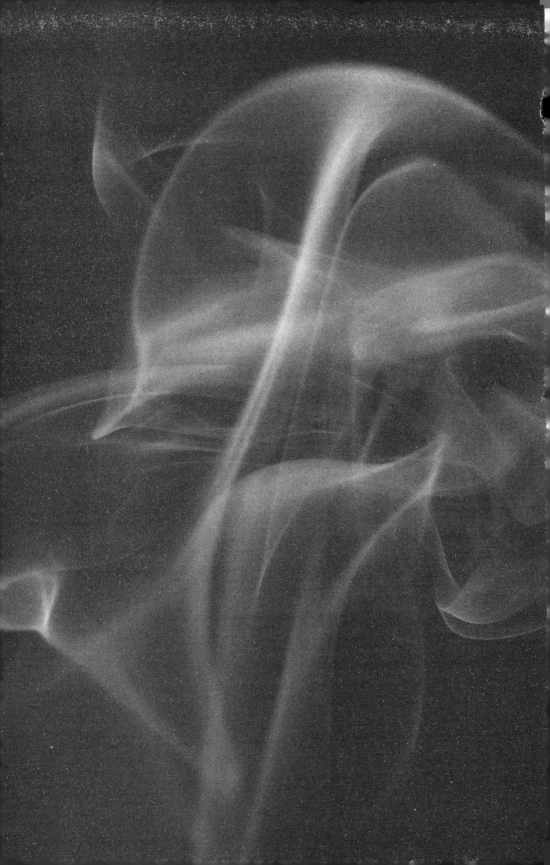

sister *of* darkness

THE CHRONICLES OF A MODERN EXORCIST

r. h. stavis

with sarah durand

DEY ST.
An Imprint of WILLIAM MORROW

HarperCollins books may be purchased for educational, business, or sales promotional use. For information, please email the Special Markets Department at SPsales@harpercollins.com.

FIRST EDITION

Designed by Paula Russell Szafranski

Library of Congress Cataloging-in-Publication Data has been applied for.

ISBN 978-0-06-265614-8

17 18 19 20 21   LSC   10 9 8 7 6 5 4 3 2 1

This book is dedicated to those who have wondered.

Those who have suffered.

Those who have thought, even for a moment,

that there might be something more.

It's for those who are willing, and ready, to see beyond the veil.

This book is dedicated to you.

CONTENTS

Introduction: The Exorcist Next Door   1

CHAPTER 1   Balled-Up Socks and Baby Dolls:
Growing Up with Demons   13

CHAPTER 2   Finally Facing My Demons   25

CHAPTER 3   Making Sense of Entities   43

CHAPTER 4   The Most Common Entities   61

CHAPTER 5   The Most Dangerous Entities of All   97

CHAPTER 6   The Source of All Things   111

CHAPTER 7   The Ins and Outs of Exorcisms   133

CHAPTER 8   Higher Beings: Spirit Guides,
Master Teachers, Ancestors, and More   147

CHAPTER 9   The Exorcism Itself   163

CHAPTER 10   Entities and Religion   189

CHAPTER 11   The Slaughterhouse Collector   193

CHAPTER 12   Exorcising the Cecil   205

CHAPTER 13   Bad Moons, Lost Souls, and
Making Sense of Everything   215

CHAPTER 14   Raising Your Frequency: The Big Picture   227

CHAPTER 15   Home Ex-Onomics   247

CHAPTER 16   Now That You Know . . .   263

Acknowledgments   *269*

sister *of* *darkness*

The Exorcist Next Door

I hate answering my phone after midnight. Like, I *really* can't stand it, and it's not because I'm worried someone I love has just died. I know a late-night call means I've got to go to work, and the job is going to be a tough one. I'm an exorcist, so I know very intimately what comes out at night, after most people go to bed. Trust me, a lot of it is pretty scary, and if you're calling me in the wee hours, you're probably face-to-face with something infinitely more terrible than you've ever seen before.

That's why, when my cell started ringing one night last year, waking me from a deep sleep, I didn't even think about letting the call go to voicemail. Somebody needed me, and they couldn't wait. When I answered, the woman on the other end of the line introduced herself as a friend of a friend, and as she continued, I could hear how scared she was.

"Something's wrong with my daughter," she whispered frantically, "and I think you're my last hope. My girl's not eating. She's always been such a happy child, so friendly to everyone, but now she's withdrawn. We've always been so close, but now she won't even tell me what's wrong. She won't tell me *anything*." She paused to take a breath, and when she next spoke I could hear her voice crack. "She's like a different child than the one I gave birth to."

I was half-asleep, but I knew what I needed to do next.

"I'm sure I can help. How old is your daughter?"

"She's only ten. She's still so young. But I'm *sure* she's possessed. Something's taken her over."

I'm used to calls like this, though they usually don't come after midnight (thank God). People contact me and tell me they've started binge drinking after years of being sober, and they can't figure out why or summon the willpower to stop. Or their marriage has turned toxic and abusive, yet they can't work up the nerve to leave. Women call me, sobbing, and say that they've been trying for years to get pregnant, and their doctors have told them to just give up and move on. Or musicians come to me complaining that they've frozen up, lost their inspiration, and are terrified to get on the stage for a huge performance. Each of these people feels fundamentally altered, like they're being pulled down by 100-pound weights or have the world's worst case of the flu. They may even look different—older and exhausted, with bags under their eyes and joints that have begun to ache and crack. They've spent thousands of dollars seeing therapists, who've listened to them patiently but come up with no workable solutions. Or they've gone to doctor after doctor, and all have sent them away, saying, "You don't have a disease or infection. There's nothing actually *wrong* with you." They may have visited an energy healer, or gone to confession to try to find some peace. But when these outlets inevitably fail, my clients start to worry that they're losing their minds. They imagine something sinister and awful has invaded the deepest part of their being. Yet how could that possibly be? People don't get "invaded." Voodoo dolls and evils spells aren't real, are they?

The truth is that something *has* taken over these totally normal, sane individuals. What I call an entity—and what people throughout history have called a demon—has attached itself or burrowed into their bodies, and now it's feeding off of them. It's living off their fears, depressions, anxieties, and a host of other negative energies and emotions. They may have had this entity with them for ten years or ten days, but it's interfering with their lives, and until it's gone things aren't going to get better. Until they find me, they don't know that I'm probably the only person in the world who can identify their problem and make it disappear.

No, I'm not the Queen of the Damned or a Goddess in Black Leather Pants. (I save the leather pants for special occasions.) I'm just Rachel Stavis, the exorcist next door.

I normally don't ask clients to come over at night. I'm not lazy; it's just that battling entities is hard, exhausting work, and if I'm not well rested, it can be tough to summon enough mental and spiritual energy to fight the way I need to. But I consider a child in peril a true emergency, so I push myself to get to work no matter how late it is.

"Please," I said to the mother on the phone, "drive here as soon as you can. Not tomorrow. Get over here right now."

About an hour later, I watched a blue minivan pull up to my house in the Valley. For those of you not familiar with Southern California, "the Valley" is shorthand for the San Fernando Valley, the sprawling patch of former orange groves just north of Los Angeles that's home to everything from the Warner Bros. lot to 99 percent of the U.S. porn industry. I could see a middle-aged woman lifting a sleeping girl out of the van's back seat, so I rushed out and met them, then walked with them to the guest cottage in my backyard.

"I'm glad you made it so quickly," I said. "Please, come inside."

The little girl opened her eyes, looked at me, then burrowed her head into the crook of her mom's shoulder. Even though I'd just barely caught a glimpse of her face, I could see how vacant her big, brown eyes were. The child who I was sure had gone to school and played happily with her friends for ten years wasn't quite there; her expression looked cloudy, almost blurry. Worse, she had something around her that only I could see: a dark puff of smoke encircling her face and head, so close it was as if it were part of her.

With her child still in her arms, the mom sat down on the big, plush couch I'd situated near the French doors that divided the front of my cottage from the room in the back. That space is my Spirit Room, where I perform all my exorcisms and do all my spiritual work. When the mom finally pulled her daughter away from her own body and shifted her just to her left, my concern for the girl doubled. Part of me even worried whether I'd be able to help her. *She's so terrified and closed off,* I thought. *Is she going to be willing enough for this exorcism to work?* The little girl still couldn't look me in the eyes, and as her mom reached toward her, she pulled away and clasped her hands between her knees.

The mom started speaking slowly, her voice shaky and soft. This isn't all that unusual; people often think they have to whisper near my Spirit Room, perhaps because it's such a calming place, with the lights low and candles flickering. Or maybe they're just worried about who might be listening, telling themselves, *If I'm quiet enough, the entities won't hear what I'm about to say.*

"When my daughter first stopped eating, we saw a few doctors and a psychiatrist. They didn't help." She started to choke up. "Then she showed me cuts and bruises on her body and swore up and down she had no idea where they'd come from. Made-up words and symbols—things that didn't make any sense—appeared on her arms and legs, and then she started talking about seeing demons." The woman was crying at this point, and I reached for a box of tissues as she continued. "Here, I'll have her show you."

The mother gently coaxed her daughter to stand up, whispering softly to her as the little girl raised up her shirt and turned around. *Good God, this breaks my heart,* I thought, eyeing the red X's that were carved into her back. The wounds weren't deep—they looked like cat scratches rather than gashes—but they were unmistakable to me. *An entity did that. To an innocent child.*

"We're religious," the mom said when her daughter returned to her side. "So when we suspected something was wrong, we talked to our priest. It started just as a friendly meeting, for counsel and prayer, like I had before I got married or after my father died. But pretty soon it turned into something different."

"How's that?" I asked, even though I knew the answer.

"He said that she might be possessed, but he couldn't tell unless he talked with her. The next day, I brought her to him after school, and he met with her for an hour or so. But instead of

doing something to help her, the priest told me she was faking."
She paused and wiped her eyes. "My baby isn't pretending. She's
just a little girl—and I know my child."

This definitely wasn't the first time I'd heard someone say
something like this. The Catholic Church has a very specific set
of guidelines about demonic possession and exorcisms, which the
Vatican updated in 1999 for the first time since 1614. According to the Church, "true" demonic possession is incredibly rare,
and they believe that most people who come to them, swearing
up and down that something's taken over them, are actually just
suffering from some terrible mental or physical ailment. In the
end, priests may say a few prayers and offer blessings, but they
still turn almost everyone away.

But because I can see entities—like the one feeding off the
ten-year-old sitting on my couch—I know they exist, and I'm
fully aware of how common they are. In fact, every single person
on this planet has probably been possessed at one point or another in their lives, and 99 percent of people are walking around
with entities now, totally oblivious to them. They may suspect
something is wrong, but they attribute it to stress, a bad boss, or
the fight they just had with their boyfriend. These traumas—big
or small—may have triggered the initial possession, but they're
symptoms, not the cause.

Shocking, huh? Don't lose any sleep over it. The fact that entities affect everything around us isn't necessarily life-or-death.
Entities are the unfortunate by-products of our topsy-turvy,
high-pressure lives that are all too often out of sync with Spirit
(the guiding spiritual force in our world). Luckily, there's a lot
you can do about them. You can prevent them from attaching
themselves to you, or if you're with me, blast them into oblivion.

I want to share with you all the truths that possessions reveal, which is exactly what I did with the terrified mom in front of me.

"Your daughter's not faking anything," I said, "and she's not sick. There's an entity attached to her, and I'm going to find out why it's there. Then, I'm going to destroy it."

Before I led the two of them into my Spirit Room, we talked for close to an hour about some recent events the girl had experienced. It turns out, she hadn't been having a good year; in fact, it had been the worst of her short life. Her beloved grandmother, who'd cared for her every day when she was a baby and toddler, had just died in a car accident. Children often think a tragedy is their fault—that they did something to deserve it or bring it on—and she was no different. She was kicking herself over all the things she should have said or done before her grandma died. She was blaming herself, believing that she should have told her grandma not to get into her car that night. This deep, intrinsic way of really *feeling* something, even if you haven't caused it, is why so many kids commit suicide when something bad happens to them. They don't yet possess the spiritual or emotional maturity to understand that everything truly *does* occur for a reason— and often we'll just never learn or understand it. Honestly, some adults never get to that place, either. Children are so innocent they can break into a million pieces over the smallest things, and that's why I always help them immediately when they're in need.

It was obvious to me that the girl's spiritual and emotional energy had dipped so low that the entity had attached to her and was now not only feeding off her depression, but also increasing her sense of regret and sadness. That's how some entities work: the worse you feel, the better off they are. They devour all the negativity you're radiating like it's an all-you-can-eat buffet, sending you into a seemingly hopeless spiritual feedback loop. I knew that if I didn't remove this entity as quickly as possible, chances were the little girl would walk around with it for the rest of her life, feeling some shade of awful every single day. If she didn't get better, the effect of the entity might even grow over time. Even worse, I understood that kids, especially very young ones like her, aren't in touch with what motivates them, so they'll spend years feeling yucky about *something*—they're just not sure what—and then make decisions out of that suffering. Eventually, the trauma—and the entity that has attached to them because of it—will have defined the course of their lives. Think about it: Did a painful experience in your childhood, like your parents' divorce or being bullied, cut you so deeply that your adult decisions are *still* based on that suffering? Do you even realize you're doing such a thing?

Children don't deserve that. *This* child certainly didn't. And that's what I was going to help her with.

I convinced the girl's mom to let me take her into my Spirit Room alone. It's dangerous to have other people close by during an exorcism because their energy may interfere with the hyperfocused flow I manipulate between my client and the entity. I also always ask tough questions during exorcisms, and most people are afraid to be honest about their deep, dark feelings if someone else is present.

The exorcism took about an hour, and it was a success; I cleared out the entities that were causing my young client's pain. Honestly, it wasn't that difficult. She was possessed by a low-level entity I call a Clive—something I'd seen many times before—combined with a higher-level entity called a Trickster. I'll describe both in vivid detail later in the book, but for now, just know that these awful beasts were amplifying the negative feelings she had about her grandmother's death, and they were making her feel crazy. They were making her *act* crazy. Worst of all, they were also committing appalling acts of physical violence against her.

I know, I know, you're probably super upset with me that I didn't describe all the gory details of the exorcism. You're probably asking yourself, *Did she vomit green bile? Did her head spin around?* Umm, no. That crazy shit only happens in the movies—most of the time. I have seen some Hollywood-level drama go down during a few of my exorcisms, and I'll talk about those and a dozen of my other exorcisms later in this book. In fact, I'll describe so many entities in the next few chapters that they'll probably feel like old, boring friends by the time you finish.

All I will say for now is that there was a happy ending. When the little girl left my house at four in the morning, she told me she felt lighter, and she looked it. She wasn't hunched over, and as she waved goodbye to me, she actually smiled. I grinned right back because I knew her sense of devastation had passed. I'd watched all that negative energy leave her body quickly, right along with the entity that had been attached to her.

Last Christmas, I ran into the girl's aunt.

"My niece is doing so well," she said happily. "She's back to her old self. She's a normal, happy kid again."

I know I sound like a narcissist, but this was no surprise. Helping people is why I do what I do. Seeing entities—and then pulling them out of people's bodies, working until there's nothing left but a gray mass that dissipates into oblivion—is why I was put on this earth, and it's going to be my job for the rest of my life. I've been seeing entities since I was just a little girl, and trust me, they were terrifying to me then. Some of them looked like something out of a horror novel, while others would blanket my room with a spiderlike web, disrupting my sleep and giving me nightmares. I didn't know what to do with what I was seeing till I was in my thirties, and then I stumbled through a lot of sloppy exorcisms until I found my groove. Believe me, when I was young, I never called what I saw or did "a gift." In fact, I thought my crazy, extrasensory ability was a curse. Now I know it's the greatest blessing I could ever ask for. It's my life's purpose.

In this book, I'll welcome you not just into my strange world, but into the entire realm of entities, Spirit, frequency, and how they directly affect you. I'll describe the many levels of entities— and what you might have attached to you right now—and show you what you can do to avoid attracting others. While you can gradually force out an entity by raising your energy level over time—or make subtle shifts in your life that will prevent the worst entities from coming to you—you can't exorcise yourself immediately. Only I can do that, right in my Spirit Room.

I'm a nondenominational exorcist, which makes a lot of people scratch their heads. *So you're an atheist?* they ask. Or they wonder: *If the entities you see aren't religious, does that mean there's no God?* That's not for me to say, really. Religious beliefs are completely personal, and faith is something *you* feel, not something I or anyone else can force upon you. I believe in what I refer to as Spirit because I tap into it every day. During exorcisms, I call in Spirit Guides, Master Teachers, angels, my ancestors, even gods and goddesses, all of whom come from and are part of Spirit. Sometimes even Jesus shows up, and it's always fun to see Buddha. You think I'm joking, don't you? Yeah, I'm not. Traditional religious figures also arise from Spirit, and in this book,

I'll talk about what Spirit is and how it affects the world around us. Spirit is often called Source (I use the two interchangeably), and it's where all good and bad things come from and return to. But you can call it Heaven, the universe, or some make-believe fairy-tale land if that's your thing.

In this book, I'll tell you stories about my life and about the exorcisms I've performed over the last decade, showing you not just that there's another world out there, surrounding each and every one of us, but that there's something you can do to protect yourself from the darker parts of that other realm. You can change your energy—which I also call frequency—to help make a better world. That, in turn, will keep entities from attaching to you—now and for the rest of your life.

I can't wait to show you how.

CHAPTER 1

Balled-Up Socks and Baby Dolls

Growing Up with Demons

My mom's name isn't Rosemary, and last I checked I wasn't growing horns, but I am certainly in a serious relationship with the dark side. I've been seeing entities my whole life. Much as your parents' faces are so familiar that you probably don't even remember the first moment you saw them, I don't recall a time when entities weren't with me. I probably even watched them floating around my crib when I was a baby.

Entities aren't beautiful creatures. Some look harmless, like puffs of smoke, but others are absolutely terrifying, with long, gaunt faces and skeletal bodies. They're sometimes gray, like cigarette ash, and you can see right through them. Some have very energetic figures, and others appear almost human, right down to their color. As scary as they all look, the way they make you feel is far more frightening. Even as an adult there are times I'll get a visitation, and the sensation of the entity in my room, near me, is so malignant that I won't get a wink of sleep the rest of the night.

If I feel that way now and can actually *comprehend* what I'm seeing, imagine what it was like to be a child experiencing these awful things. At first I'd only feel their negativity near me, but then I began to actually witness them. Some of my earliest memories involve seeing shadowy figures on the walls, under my bed, or in closets. But unlike the shadow puppets that lots of kids like to make, these monsters were real—and they didn't resemble animals or humans. I'd hide under the sheets, shaking, so I wouldn't see them, and then I'd cry quietly to myself, worried my mom would scold me if she knew I was still awake.

When I was about nine, these phantomlike visions became clearer and more well formed, with recognizable features, like I see them now. I think Spirit waited to reveal them fully till I was more mature because it wanted to ease me into my gift. Spirit was trying to give me a psychic recess rather than a final exam. Entities didn't try to attach to me when I was young, either. I don't exactly know why, but again, I think Spirit was protecting me somehow. It knew what my life plan was well before I did, so it was slowly introducing me to it.

Still, being so young, I couldn't forget what I'd been seeing, and I was petrified. These strange visions weren't warm or friendly; they were dark, unwelcome strangers in my personal space, and they made me feel nauseated, clammy, and hollow inside. I imagined I'd done something awful to deserve them—

even though I couldn't figure out what—and I felt dirty and ashamed.

I have two particularly vivid childhood memories of entities—one deeply disturbing and one not so much. I'll start with the one that won't make you sleep with the lights on.

When I was a child, I used to ball my socks up and store them in a drawer. Once, when I was ten or eleven and getting ready for school, I picked out a pair, one wrapped around the other, and threw them on my bed. Then I turned around and walked toward my closet to choose my outfit for the day. After I'd pulled on jeans and a T-shirt, I did a 180 toward my bed, ready to sit down and put on my socks. I looked up and saw something that made me stop in my tracks: lying there, side by side in perfect formation—and not in the ball I'd so carefully rolled them into just a few days before—were my socks.

I was shocked and scared, of course. Why wouldn't I be? I wasn't even out of elementary school, and I was supposed to be picking dandelions in the playground, not getting visitations from ghosts—or whatever it was that had done this. These naughty little tricks started happening more regularly after that, too. I'd walk into my bathroom and see lipstick smeared on the mirror, or I wouldn't be able to find my set of keys, which I always put in the same place every single day. Entities don't do these sorts of things to me anymore—possibly because now, in my thirties, I can communicate with them, and they don't feel the need to dance around to get my attention. But years ago, they happened *all* the time.

For every visitation that was silly or spooky, though, there were just as many that were malevolent. One of the worst happened around the same time as the sock incident.

One night I was sound asleep, and I began dreaming that I was holding something close to me. It was unclear what it was exactly, but it felt like a doll. When I turned it toward me, so I could get a good look, I saw that it was just an average baby doll, with long hair, a pink dress, long eyelashes, and lips pursed in a perfect O.

I was born in Los Angeles in the late 1970s, but my mom and I moved to South Florida when I was two. I'm a child of the eighties, and my bedroom had one of those large stereo systems with a pair of tape decks, a receiver, a turntable, and massive rectangular speakers. The whole setup was probably four feet high, and the console showed the time in bright sea green, so at night my whole room looked like it had been coated in glow-in-the-dark algae.

I'm not sure what it was that woke me up, but suddenly, I bolted straight up in my bed. *Oh, man. What a weird dream. Why in the world was I sleeping with that strange baby doll?* I was never the type of girl who played with dolls, as you may have gathered by now.

As I cleared my eyes, I looked over, and in the glow of the green light, I saw something next to me. It was the shape and size of the doll, but it was the least innocent thing I'd seen in my life. Instead, it was this *creature*—a baby creature—but with sharp, exposed teeth. It was grimacing at me. The sweet blond doll of my dreams had morphed into something heinous.

That's the first real moment I remember shutting my eyes tight, covering them with my hands, and screaming silently to myself, *This is not happening. This is not real. None of this is true because, if it is, I can't bear to breathe.*

When I finally pulled my hands away from my face and

opened my eyes, the doll had disappeared. Somehow, by denying her very existence, I had willed her away. At that very moment, I learned that I had the power to shut out these awful beings, whatever they were, and prevent myself from seeing them.

The problem was that I wasn't always successful. I'd tell myself that I was imagining them, or I'd look at the entities directly and silently yell, *You are not real! Go away!* But when I was done with my tirade, the beasts would sometimes still be there. I was helpless. And worse, I had no hope; there was never, ever, a way for me to make them stop coming to me altogether.

At first, the entities didn't visit me every night. Instead, they came every few days, usually showing themselves as shadows that weren't necessarily human-shaped, but still noticeable. Even though I couldn't really make out exactly what they were, though, I could feel them. I sensed that they were malevolent and harmful even though I couldn't exactly tell what they were *doing*.

I began to differentiate between types of entities, and I'd see them walking or floating next to total strangers, or attached to a friend of mine. Unfortunately, at times I'd watch an entity I now call a Wraith following children on the playground, their shadows appearing before I could make out their forms. I didn't understand it then, but Wraiths are attracted to people who've suffered sexual abuse. Realizing this now, I'm so sad for these children I once knew.

The entities I saw attached to other people never tried to spook me like the entities who visited me, and, in fact, I'm not even sure they realized I could see them. For example, when I was about nine, and the shadows I saw were becoming more defined, I was friends with a girl who had a Wraith attached to her. My friend once tried to touch me sexually, and I pulled back, disgusted. *What is wrong with her?* I thought. I now understand that she wasn't in control of herself; she was being sexually abused, a Wraith had attached to her, and it was showing and expressing itself through her, completely oblivious to the fact that I could see it.

Outside of my room at night, entities were just *there*. In social situations when I had to focus, like in class, I'd try to tune them out, and soon, it worked. I became skilled at this. I'd will them away, feel the tiniest bit of confidence, and pretend to have a normal life.

In reality, I was anything but normal.

People who experience physical or emotional abuse or trauma or witness something unspeakable often retreat into their own minds and detach, so they don't feel what's happening. Disconnection and denial can be powerful coping mechanisms, but the problem is, they only work for a short time. They don't make the problem go away, and worse, they perpetuate it. The longer you keep peeling off a scab rather than letting it fully heal, the worse your scar will become. In order for a person to be able to handle an extreme situation or encounter, they either need to have the emotional and psychological capacity to deal with it—or enlist the help of someone who does.

Because I was so young, I couldn't process what was happening to me, or reconcile my reactions. I was innocent and psychologically pure, and being bombarded every single day and night by terrifying things was the equivalent of throwing black paint on a white wall. I needed an adult to help me.

The most likely candidate would have been my mother, but she was battling other kinds of demons. My mom had kidnapped me from my dad—boarding a plane out of LA without even telling him she was leaving him—and she divorced him when we settled in Florida. I didn't have much of a relationship with my dad after the split, and the closest family I had was my mother. I first confided in her when I was around seven years old.

"Mom," I said, "there are scary monsters in my room. They won't go away."

She was so cold.

"There are no such things as monsters, Rachel. Stop making things up."

Her words cut me then, and each additional time I'd bring up what I was seeing, the pain and shame of her dismissal got worse. She'd shut me down, and I'd feel even more wounded. *Why doesn't she believe me?* And as I got older, I grew angry, and my response evolved into, *Even if she doesn't understand me, why won't she at least be sympathetic to how I'm feeling?*

It took me a long time to come to grips with this, but the fact is that my mother had a lot of mental problems. She was a malignant narcissist, meaning that she wasn't happy unless she was making someone else unhappy. I'm not even sure why she left my father, and I never asked because she was so vindictive toward both of us that she'd never tell me the full truth. Talking to my mother was always a superficial exercise, so getting to the root of anything emotional or deep was next to impossible.

I loved my stepdad, whom my mom married when I was eight, but he fell into the role of enabler. He refused to confront her when she was being nasty, and when my mom had tantrums, he would just let her scream. She'd get mad if my stepdad or I didn't compliment her in a certain way, or she'd lash out if we didn't perform tasks exactly when she wanted us to, in the exact manner she demanded. She'd even become enraged if she goaded you into fighting with her and you wouldn't. She'd fly off the handle if she was critical and mean and you didn't get upset or cry, and she'd melt down if I accomplished something or if someone complimented me in front of her. I used to close my bedroom door because I couldn't deal with her energy, and eventually she got so angry about this that she made my stepdad take my door of its hinges. She ripped my posters off my walls and broke my things, but my stepdad didn't intervene because he didn't want to cross her. He, like everyone, was afraid of her.

I'm almost positive my mom had Munchausen syndrome. She was always convinced there was something wrong with her, so she'd run to the doctor and come back with either no diagnosis or a set of possible illnesses she'd make a huge fuss about, only to set up another series of appointments with specialists. When those didn't prove helpful, she'd try an elective surgery or opt for injections of one kind or another. These put her in so much pain that she began popping painkillers, and pretty soon, she was a hard-core opioid addict. She hid her addiction from me and my brother—the child she had with my stepdad—and I didn't learn about this until I was an adult. But even if I'd known when I was young, nothing would have been different. I didn't have the maturity to understand or manage a problem that complicated when I was a kid. All I thought was that my mother was a highly selfish, emotionally erratic person who didn't love me half as much as I needed her to. Now, though, it all makes sense. Mom was under the sway of something bigger than her.

Mom always had dark clouds around her. I tried to block them out, but they were so obvious I never could. She'd been raped as a child—though she never talked about it—and I now realize she had a terrible Wraith attached to her. It makes me sad to think about this, honestly. On the surface, my mom was a strong person, and if she hadn't faced so many difficulties she could have been a real force to be reckoned with. But the fact that her issues were so overpowering made her childish, always in need of mothering herself.

For instance, my stepdad passed away when I was sixteen, and Mom became afraid to go to sleep. She'd wake me up in the middle of the night and beg me to stay up with her until she drifted off, regardless of whether I had school the next day. She also began having panic attacks during this intense period of grief, and I had to talk her through them.

I got no love or even the smallest bit of kindness in return, though. She once took me to a ballet for a "nice" evening with a friend of hers, and, for no reason at all, I started to panic when I walked inside. I asked Mom to go back outside with me.

"Suck it up," she spat at me as she turned away. "You're embarrassing me."

Caretaker was my only role when I was with her, and it forced me to become an adult at a very early age.

The only time I ever truly felt like a kid was with my grandmother. Because Mom was so needy and incapable of taking care of herself, she'd always insisted that we live close to her parents. Our house was about thirty minutes away from my grandparents, and for my entire life, my grandma was basically a saint to me. She would have done absolutely anything to make me happy, which was the complete opposite of my mother. My grandma would sit with me at dinner and say, "Rach, tell me about your day. Every little bit." She'd get on her hands and knees and play Legos with me. She taught me empathy and basic human connection, and ultimately, I think she made me into the person I am today.

My grandma's only big flaw was that she enabled my mom, too. She was just as afraid of her as everyone else was, so she'd dance around her, worrying that my mom would lash out at her or stop talking to her if she was angry. I was her only comfort against my mom, so she let me stay with her as often as I liked—for as long as I wanted. Unfortunately, because I was forcing myself to believe that what I was seeing was all in my imagination—which my mother reinforced—I never felt brave enough to talk to my grandmother about my experiences with the entities. I thought what I was seeing made me strange. I didn't want to be judged, even by the person who loved and understood me most in the world, so I thought it was better to keep my mouth shut.

I'm not sure if my grandmother saw entities. I never asked her, and she passed away when I was in my late twenties, so I never had the chance to talk to her while she was alive. Because she was so dismissive of me when I told her, I'm sure my mother didn't have this gift. So, when people ask me now where my extrasensory abilities came from, I don't have an exact answer. I was just born this way, and I deeply believe this is what I'm meant to do in this life.

There may be other people out there exactly like me, but unfortunately, I've never had the chance to meet them. I know individuals who have similar gifts—like oracles, mediums, and shamans—but they work in general energy healing, meaning that they clean the body *and* spirit. Demons are what I do, and that involves a very specific type of energy focus. I've only met one other person who may have a similar ability to mine, someone I'll tell you about later in this book. I hope to help this man try to learn his gifts. But if there's a little girl in Iowa or Japan or Mexico reading this, thinking, *Finally, I know I'm not alone,* I hope she comes to understand that what she's seeing might be scary, but there's a way to use it to help those in need. Your power may feel like too much to bear now, but you *will* be able to harness it for good.

I spend a lot of time speaking to Source and all sorts of Higher Beings, including Spirit Guides, Master Teachers, angels, and more, and I'll describe them in detail later. Just know for now that they are my most trusted guides not just in my life, but in all the exorcisms I do. Most of the time, I don't even specifically request a particular being from Spirit. I just ask for help, and it responds however it sees fit. Together, Spirit and these Higher Beings form what I consider my belief system: that all things good and bad—or high frequency and low frequency—spring from Spirit, and they cause and direct everything we do in this world. There are no accidents: it's just Source and all its beings forging a path and affecting all of us. The good news is that if we learn to listen to Spirit, like I have, we can be at peace with that.

Though Spirit has never out-and-out said it, I believe I was chosen to have this gift because it was known that I could be trusted to bring it out into the world. I never understood that as a child—I didn't even know what was happening to me—but now, as an adult, I see there's a method to all of this. Before I was even born, Spirit knew I could manage my powers. After years and years of denial, shame, anger, grief, and frustration, I now grasp what to do with my abilities. My dysfunctional, desperately lonely childhood helped make me strong, and that's the attitude I use when I face entities. I don't take shit from them. I go into situations that other people would run away from, even with fifty other people holding their hands and cheering them on. I barge right in alone, fearlessly, and I do my job. I take what I once thought was a curse and turn it into a blessing. It's a way to help people better their lives.

That's exactly what I want to do in this book.

CHAPTER 2

Finally Facing My Demons

Most kids who are raised in dysfunctional households become pathological caretakers. I'm no exception; it's part of my genetic makeup to help anyone and everyone, especially because I know what's hurting them.

There are a few problems with having this kind of excessive compassion, though. First, those who are wired this way often think of others—almost obsessively—before themselves, noticing everyone else's problems while denying their own. I did this *all* the time, for years. I remember being at day camp one summer, and as I walked past the nurse's station I noticed a sick boy sitting with his head between his legs. Down around his head swirled a dark cloud—the telltale sign that an entity had attached to him. I knew that if I looked closer, I'd be able to see its form. My heart stopped, and I was desperate to run to this poor boy's side. *I know what's really wrong with you,* I wanted to say. *I need you to know I'm here for you.* I hadn't even sought out help for my *own* problems, yet all I wanted to do was save him.

Second, when a pathological caretaker looks for someone to care for, they tend to seek out the most damaged, neediest people they can find. That was my specialty. I lived with a woman who was desperate for attention, so I was used to that kind of behavior, and I sought out more of it. But the friends I found and surrounded myself with didn't just *seem* troubled. A lot of times, I knew they really *were* troubled, not just by trauma or grief but because of the terrible entities they'd attracted.

By the time I got to middle school, I was exhausted. So many of my friendships flamed out in a destructive cycle that involved me trying too hard to help the other person, but in the end, them running all over me. My best friend was named Anne, and her mom smoked too much pot and paid more attention to her boyfriend than she did to her own daughter. Anne was depressed because of it, so she spent more time out with me than she did at home. Then, one day, she stopped returning my calls. I hadn't done anything to anger or alienate her; she'd just decided to move on to a new group of friends.

I finally decided at the age of thirteen that it would just be easier if I detached from everyone and kept my distance. So, I transformed myself from the caring, supportive friend to all into a complete loner, the weird kid walking down the halls, dressed in black with my head down and my hair in my eyes. Everyone now gossiped about how strange I'd become, but they all stayed away.

As high school approached, though, the world changed. It

was the 1990s, and piercings, tattoos, and black Doc Martens were everything. I listened to Alice in Chains and Faith No More and loved the movie *The Craft*, which was about four high school girls who happened to be witches. Suddenly being different was cool. My peers now thought I was mysterious and "alternative," and I found a posse of fellow weirdos who welcomed me with open arms. Within that group, I met a boy named Kevin. He was a flannel-wearing, guitar-playing, dark, broody boy who was into drugs, and I developed a huge crush on him right away. We soon became "best friends," though all the while I wanted more.

Kevin was deeply troubled. And I fell right into my old role of caretaker. I wanted to do everything I could to save him from his self-harm and self-loathing. Between my abusive upbringing and my natural ability, pathological caretaking was comfortable to me, and I felt my only value was to do everything I could for everyone—especially for people I thought I loved. But even though Kevin and I were as close as could be, I didn't feel right telling him what I thought was at the root of all of his problems, or how to fix them. I just wanted to be there for him—all the time—and revel in his darkness. Misery loves company, right? He was burdened with entities. Of course he was. But my mom's cold rejection had taught me to shut my mouth about all of that. Sure, being edgy was great and all, but even goth teenagers had limits.

Like most people with entities, Kevin couldn't change. He was stuck in a well of unhappiness and couldn't figure out how to climb out. Nor did he want to, either. I think he accepted being dysfunctional and unhappy and wore it like a beat-up leather jacket. I could see entities around him, and I realized they were doing something harmful to him, but I still didn't understand the extent of their powers. I hadn't yet figured out what motivated them, or exactly what particular brand of havoc they could wreak in which particular ways. All I knew was that Kevin was plagued more than most people, and that drew me to him like a moth to flame.

Our friendship was intense, but rocky. It followed a pattern: He'd get a girlfriend, and I'd become livid. In retaliation, I'd get a boyfriend, and when he found out he'd fly into a jealous rage. The back-and-forth madness soon became too much, and Kevin and I stopped talking.

Then my stepfather—who'd endured my mom's craziness, and who I loved because of that and so many other things—died suddenly from a heart attack when I was sixteen. I approached Kevin, begging him to be someone he wasn't able to be: a sane, compassionate man who could help me through my grief. I needed him to dig deep, to show me some sympathy, but quickly I realized he wasn't capable. This ended our friendship for good.

Kevin called me years later, when I was in college.

"I dropped out of school," he said. "I went to rehab because I was addicted to pills. I'm trying to stay clean and sober now."

We hadn't spoken in over four years, but hearing his voice and this news made me so sad. Deep down, I'd always *known* this was going to be Kevin's path. Maybe I didn't predict exactly what would make his life so difficult, but I had felt in my bones that he would not know peace. Yet even with my Superwoman complex, I also realized I never would have saved him. Sure, I was the girl who wanted to rescue every homeless person and abandoned kitten I saw on the street, but by my early twenties, I'd told myself that it wasn't my job. I was trying to be normal. So I ignored entities and focused on my life and career. I left

Florida, moved around the country, and settled in Denver, where I started writing under the name R. H. Stavis.

I spent most of the early 2000s creating comics, graphic novels, scripts for video games, and screenplays for television. Writing for a living had always been my dream because it was the perfect way to escape reality, and I'd spent hours during my childhood holed up in my room, making up stories to escape my terrible existence with my mom. Back in the day, horror and gaming were male-dominated industries, so I had some issues trying to break in, but I was determined—and it paid off. I soon created the backstory for *Lara Croft, Tomb Raider,* got invitations to speak at major comic and gaming conventions across the country, and developed scripts for a few feature films.

I also published my first novel, *Daniel's Veil.* As the saying goes, "Write what you know," so even though I was still forcing myself to reject the notion of entities, all the fiction I created was born from what I'd seen. I never called anything "an entity" in my stories, but I wrote a lot about Source and the afterlife, as well as shapeshifting bodies, intuition, and feelings. I think writing fiction was a form of therapy for me. There are other dimensions (like the etheric realm and Source) that people don't understand—and at the time, I didn't fully grasp them, either— but bringing them to life in my novels brought me closer.

I made what I thought were great friends, and I fell in love and married a man who I believed was all I'd ever need. But our relationship was totally superficial. I didn't tell my husband about my secret vision, hiding my real self from him. We fought all the time, and I left him after a few years.

I loved Denver and thought the Rockies were the most gorgeous things I'd ever seen, but I'd always been drawn to Los

Angeles. It was probably because I was born there, and it was definitely because it was far away from Florida and all the terrible memories I had of my mother and my childhood. In fact, my mother passed away a few years before my divorce. She'd developed stomach cancer and died six weeks after her diagnosis. I hadn't even known she was sick until my brother texted me a few days after she was gone, and I decided not to go to her funeral. *Why attend a lie?* I thought. *Mom was never, ever kind to me.* We hadn't spoken in years, and now she was gone. My mother. Her death left a hollow self-loathing in my gut that would take years of emotional work to fill.

I finally moved to Los Angeles in 2009. My career had started to accelerate, and I'd often have to hop on a plane in Denver, fly down to LA for a day or two, crash on a friend's couch, then fly back. After months of doing that I decided it made a lot more sense for me to be in a place where I didn't have to schedule meetings days or weeks in advance. Instead, I could go see anyone at a moment's notice, grab a coffee or a drink whenever someone asked. I said to myself, *I'm just going to move there, find a place, and figure things out from there.*

As soon as I left Denver, my career opened up—but my personal life still hadn't. When I easily could have found happy, healthy people to surround myself with, I was having relationship problems with everyone, and I was miserable because I couldn't resolve any of the issues I'd had with my mom or in my childhood. I felt like I was hiding who I was all the time, and it had become a huge burden. I was desperate and all alone in the world.

Then, one day, I was driving through my neighborhood and had stopped at an intersection. As I moved slowly through it, another car came out of nowhere and broadsided me. Neither I nor the other driver was injured, and my car was hardly damaged, but for a full week, I felt like I'd been slapped in the face. When I woke up in the morning, all I could think about was the crunching sound of my car's back door caving in and the feeling of my neck snapping to the right.

I've spent my whole life trying to micromanage everything, I thought, *and then some asshole hit me out of the blue.* Suddenly, it dawned on me that I'd been so busy doing everything in my power to control the world around me, and then life had spun violently away from me in a split second. Something inside me woke up, shifted, and released itself, and I started to realize that it was time to surrender and let go. I had to open up my spirit to whatever life had to offer—good or bad. I'd stop pushing entities away; I'd face them head-on. I'd work against them and try to make them disappear from the lives of those they plagued. I wanted to share my gift. I needed to come out of the shadows. I wanted to help people, but I wouldn't start until the right person and the right time came along.

Within a year or so, I found my moment.

I met a man named Peter through my work, and we soon started dating. We got serious quickly and moved in together. Pete was very into spirituality, and we connected over this. More than almost anything, he wanted to learn Reiki, which is a spiritually guided healing technique that involves a person channeling bad energy from the body, and good energy into it, through touch. Given what I do now, which involves manipulating energy, you might assume I'd be drawn to Reiki, but I wasn't. Reiki just didn't hold any interest for me because it was too touchy-feely. Too flowery, bell-bottom, groovy. I'm totally open to positive healing, but only in concrete, tangible ways that I can see. Reiki is all about weird, *invisible* forces, and that just isn't my thing.

"Sorry, I don't give a shit about Reiki," I said.

Peter wasn't convinced. "No, you're coming with me. You have to try this. It's very spiritual. You'll enjoy it."

Peter often tried to sell me on things he knew I'd hate, like the time he tried to take me camping (I'm a glamping kind of woman), or the day he begged me to go to a five-day music festival that had no indoor toilets. This time, however, I suspected his intentions weren't totally selfish, so I caved.

"You know what? If you're really into this, I'll go with you. But you are going to owe me."

One weekend morning, we drove to a friend of a friend's apartment a few miles away. When we walked in the front door, there were six or seven people I didn't know sitting in a circle, with the lights low and candles burning, sipping tea. It was eleven in the morning and the sun was so bright outside I still had my sunglasses on. They all looked as if they'd just gotten home from Burning Man. I'm Goth Barbie. This was not my crowd.

"Today's going to be beautiful," some super flowery stranger said, reaching out to touch my arm. "Reiki is pure love."

"Ummm . . . okay," I said, turning my head to roll my eyes. *Fuck this,* I whispered to myself.

I settled into a love seat on the outer edge of the crowd. One of the strangers who'd been seated on the floor stood up and smiled. "Good morning, everyone. I'll be leading things today. First, I need someone to volunteer for treatment."

Peter, who was always the life of the party, the guy who'd never met a stranger, jumped up immediately.

"That's me. I'd be happy to."

"Great," the teacher responded a little too enthusiastically. "Please come and lie down over here."

This woman had set up what looked like a massage table in one corner of the room. She motioned Pete over, and he climbed right up and made himself comfortable, lying on his back. When the teacher called the rest of us and asked us to join her, the remaining people in the room didn't hesitate. They surrounded the table in perfect formation. But I hung back a few inches, regretting with all of my being the moment I'd agreed to come here.

The teacher cupped her palms and positioned them over my boyfriend's body. Then she asked us to do the same.

"You," she said, nodding at me. "Place your hands over his core. We need to get the energy flowing."

By its very definition, the core is the center of your being and the seat of many of your emotions. Many people hold tension in their bellies, literally stomaching their pain, and when someone's nervous about something, they'll often experience nausea. The core is where energy is held most powerfully by most people—where the "root" of emotional issues and traumas lie. Now that I've been a practicing exorcist for almost a decade, I work with the core all the time because it's where entities typically feed from. They may not show themselves directly *in* the core, but they feast off the abundance of energy in it.

Standing in that hippie's LA living room that day, though, I had no idea what I was doing or why I had to put my cupped palms two inches over my date's now-half-naked body. But I did as I was told, and when I looked down, I saw something.

Holy shit, I thought. *There's one of those creatures in there.*

My hands had instantly started shaking, and I pulled them away from him as fast as I could. The closest door I could see led out to a small balcony, so I turned around, practically leaped through that door, closed the curtains behind me, and stepped outside. As soon as I hit fresh air I started gasping. For the next ten minutes or so, while everyone else stood around my boyfriend and manipulated his energy, I paced.

Of course, I'd seen entities before—and I knew Peter had them just like anyone—but this time was different. I'd suddenly fully grasped exactly what was inside him and what it could do. Even though Peter was extremely outgoing, he was sometimes quick to anger, and now I understood why. His volatility was because of this entity.

Even more than coming to terms with the entities' power, though, I'd realized who I was—and I wasn't sure I liked it. I wanted to be normal, in a regular relationship, but that was never going to be the case. Admitting who I was—and all that that entailed—was the last nail in the coffin. I knew I could never go back from that moment on.

After what felt like hours, Peter came outside, looking entirely confused.

"What happened in there?"

Now, Peter knew a fair bit about me by then, but I hadn't told him about seeing entities. I was still too scared of being rejected, judged, or told I was insane. I'd fallen for this man, and letting him into that part of my life felt too dangerous. But I was still shaking, and Peter was looking at me, desperate for an explanation and half-worried that I was about to jump off that fourth-floor balcony. It was no time to lie.

"Listen, this is going to sound absolutely nuts," I said. "And I won't be offended if you break up with me because of what I'm about to say. But I see these strange things, like, I don't know, *de-*

mons or something, all the time. Usually they're floating around people or attached to them, but I just saw one inside you. Right in your stomach. It was feeding off of you."

I shut my eyes and gritted my teeth, bracing for his reaction. I knew it would not be good. No one had ever responded well to this before.

He didn't run in the other direction at all.

"Tell me what it looked like."

I took a breath, almost in shock, and then started speaking. "Well, to me, it looked like a child's drawing of a ghost. Sort of a cloaked blob, with no arms and legs, lines for eyes, and a squiggly mouth. It was Casper the Unfriendly Ghost, but gray."

I looked up at him, and his eyes grew wide.

"You're not crazy. It makes complete sense."

"What makes sense?"

"When I was little," he said, "I used to draw something just like that when I was having a hard time with life or suffering in some way. It was a little ghost, and I'd always ask it to protect me. When I walked into this apartment today, I was feeling vulnerable, just as I did when I was a kid."

There are times in our lives that are mapped out energetically, and we'll never fully understand how or why they are. It didn't matter that I didn't know why Peter was feeling vulnerable. He didn't have to tell me. All that mattered was that he was in the midst of a preordained awakening—and so was I.

"Did you think about that ghost when you came here?"

He paused and considered my question for a minute. "No, I haven't thought about that in years. But now that I am, it feels like an old friend. Honestly, I feel better now."

I didn't want to be the bearer of bad news, but I had no choice.

"Look," I said, "that friendly little ghost is still with you, but he's not protecting you. He's feeding off of you. He's a parasite and you're his host."

Before Peter's Reiki session, I'd never made this connection. I hadn't realized what entities were doing to the people they'd attached to. I suppose I'd been too frightened of what I was seeing to really study them. But when I watched the entity pulsating inside my boyfriend's stomach, watching something flow from his body into this strange gray blob, it all clicked into place. Entities gorge on the energy of humans.

Peter became as pale as his little ghost friend.

"What the hell am I supposed to do?" he shouted. "I want this damn thing out of me!"

Peter was desperate. Here was a man I cared for, and he was being plagued. Only I knew what was attacking him, sucking his energy away like a feasting vampire. For the first time in my life, I realized what I needed to do next. I wasn't going to pretend the entity wasn't there or try to will it away. My sweet boyfriend was possessed by a demon, and I had to cast it out of his body.

I just had no idea how.

When I perform exorcisms now, I work in my Spirit Room, with burning candles and herb blends that I choose specifically for the situation, crystals placed strategically in every corner, and visual and tactile aids of all sorts that put my clients at ease. They include pillows, soft blankets, and candles, as well as religious artwork from many different kinds of religions. All of this combines to make it simpler for me to remove the entities from their bodies. But it took me years of trial and error to find just the right setting, tools, and atmosphere to do my work. My first exorcism was *nothing* like what I do today. Then, the only thing I knew for sure was that I had to remove the entity from Pete's body, and that I had the power to do so.

I suppose I'd had the intuition and strength to remove entities for years. But, again, I'd been reluctant to step into who I was. I'd been trying to rationalize my "gift" away for so many years, trying to blend in instead of standing out. If I actually performed an exorcism, I was officially declaring that I wouldn't try to disappear anymore. It was a huge step, and I was going to take it.

My first issue was where to perform the exorcism. I decided I needed as much room to work as possible, with lots of light, so I made up my mind I'd stay outside while Pete lay down in a small room inside. He could rest comfortably while I tried to do this thing I'd never done before. The fact that I believed—for my very first exorcism—that I would be successful while far away from a client, where I couldn't sense their energy or see the entity in their body, is ridiculous to me now. Today, I know that the best way to help someone is to be right there beside them, using all my power and strength to fight what's attached to them.

But that afternoon, while Peter lay on his back and I bumbled around in our backyard, I closed my eyes and asked Spirit to send me support.

And sure enough, as soon as I opened my eyes, I felt the presence of my aids, whom I'll discuss in detail later. They included Hecate (a Greek goddess), the Archangel Michael, and a Spirit Guide.

Then, I closed my eyes again and pictured the entity inside Peter leaving his body. I summoned all of my mental and spiritual strength and, with the Higher Beings surrounding me, willed the entity to stop feeding off him and leave. Over and over in my head, I said, *Leave. Go back where you came from. Or die.* Sweat started to pour down my face, but I kept my focus, repeating my words and staying connected to the Higher Beings at the same time. About an hour later, I suddenly started to relax. The tension left my shoulders, and I began to feel a shift in the energy around me. I visualized my boyfriend's body lying on the bed inside the house, and, in my mind, he looked different. The blackness that had been inside him was now gone.

I walked inside and approached Peter, still flat on his back.

"How do you feel?"

"Different," he said. "Lighter."

"What was it like?" I was desperate to know what he'd experienced as I worked outside.

"I felt sick most of the time, like I was going to throw up. But I didn't." He paused, sat up, and looked me straight in the eyes. "I could feel the energy around me shifting. The whole atmosphere in the room changed."

That night, Peter and I went to bed early, and he slept like a rock. When he woke the next morning, he told me he'd dreamed that a woman came through our bedroom window, put her hands on his stomach, and removed something.

"What did she look like?" I asked.

"She was a small cloaked figure," he said. "She was tiny and dressed entirely in black."

Of course, I thought as I nodded my head. *It was Hecate.* I'd called her in the day before, recognizing her through her very specific energetic vibration. Peter's description matched her perfectly.

Even better, Peter told me that afternoon that for the first time in his adult life he'd started the day without a single negative thought in his head. He felt completely optimistic and grateful to be alive.

Unfortunately, I didn't. Even though I'd helped free someone I deeply cared for of all the negative forces that had been weighing him down for as long as he could remember, I felt heavy and clouded. Sure, I'd finally interacted with the entities and made one person's life better, but I was as burdened as I'd ever been. I knew I'd turned a corner and couldn't ignore my gift anymore—but what was I going to do with it?

It wouldn't take me long to find out.

When I first moved to Los Angeles, I had crossed paths with a man named Durek. Durek is now a world-renowned, third-generation shaman who travels the world healing people, but when I met him, he was spending most of his time in Los Angeles.

Now, you're likely thinking, *But I thought you were skeptical of all that woo-woo stuff?* Let me clarify. Even though I've never been drawn to modern energy work like Reiki, I've always been motivated by spirituality. I talk to Spirit all the time, after all. The difference between what I do and practices like Reiki is pronounced to me; while energy work is something that's evolved only recently, spiritual practices like shamanism are ancient. They're more in line with what I do.

I liked to spend time with Durek, so one night, I had him over for dinner. We were talking about the idea of past lives, exploring whether or not we felt we'd had them (we're both sure we have). I was just the tiniest bit tipsy, not even close to being drunk, when suddenly, my sights opened up. Light blasted in, and I felt like I'd just gotten twenty-twenty vision after being half-blind for years. *What is going on?* I thought as Durek kept talking, seemingly oblivious to the fact that I felt like a Technicolor bomb had just exploded in front of me.

Then the floodgates of my mind opened up.

Out of nowhere, entities swarmed toward me and crowded around me. Remember that scene in *The Birds*, when Tippi Hedren and Rod Taylor tear down a rural road, swarmed by thousands of crows? That's how I felt at my dinner table, only worse. Entities were *everywhere*, in all sizes and all colors, banging on my limbs, whispering in my ears, pushing into my chest, and reaching their tentacles toward my eyeballs. Some swirled around my head, around and around and around till I was dizzy and had to look away. One crawled out of the refrigerator, hissed at me, and then shut the door behind it as it zipped into the air.

I was too paralyzed to say anything to Durek. I silently begged the entities to go away, but I couldn't stop them from coming in.

The next three days were pure hell. Everywhere I turned, there were entities. I saw thousands of what I now call Clives, the smallest of the entities, who always come in shades of gray or green and always have recognizable facial features even if their bodies are often blobs. I watched the entity I call the Sandman casting a spiderweb across entire neighborhoods. I saw harmless entities like the Furby, who has giant eyes and a cotton-candy body. Many of these entities were either floating through the air or attempting to push inside me, but they were also attached to people. I saw homeless men screaming obscenities, a sure sign that they'd been possessed, and a businessman walking by with his shoulders slumped, as if plagued by deep depression. When I looked closer, I could see instead that it was an entity, its formless body sitting on his shoulders, with tubes reaching into his core.

My world was turned on its head. I'd be walking down Hollywood Boulevard, bustling with tourists taking photos and restaurants spilling patrons onto the street, when suddenly the blue sky above me would turn into a swarming mass of hideous creatures only I could see. Again and again I tried to will them away, but nothing happened. For three straight days, I was helpless.

My boyfriend was incredibly supportive, but he didn't have any answers. Being alone didn't help, either. I soon realized I needed to be honest with myself. I needed to be candid, to become *me*. No more hiding from who I was. No more silence.

For the first time in my life, I really, truly opened up about who and what I was.

"I think I'm losing my mind," I said to a friend. "There are these hideous *things* floating around, and of course I've seen them before, actually, I've known about them my whole life, but now I can't ignore them. I can't block them from my sight and make them go away!"

My friends almost all work in creative fields, so they're fairly liberal, open-minded types who aren't taken aback by crazy stories. Sure, I could have been telling them the plot of my next horror novel, but I was so earnest that I'm fairly certain they all believed me. At the very least, they were sympathetic.

But there was absolutely nothing any of them could do to help change my circumstances. I reached out to Durek, finally able to be honest with him, but just like everyone else, he couldn't take my gift away. All he or anyone else said was: "It's time for you to use it."

After three days of not being able to accept their advice, I was so exhausted that I poured myself a huge glass of bourbon and decided to have a heart-to-heart with Spirit.

"Okay, listen," I said firmly. "I know I'm always asking you for help, but this time it's different. I really need you to tell me what's going on. I promise you, I want to figure out how to move forward, and what to do with my ability. No more running away."

As it always does, Spirit responded almost immediately. In a voice just above a whisper, I heard: *You're either going to lose your mind completely in a matter of days, or use your skill to help many people.*

Obviously, checking yourself into an insane asylum isn't an appealing choice, so I chose the latter. And my life has never been the same.

CHAPTER 3

Making Sense of Entities

L os Angeles is a town where people are open to just about anything: hot yoga, healing crystals, cryogenic chamber therapy . . . the list goes on. So, when I started telling friends that I'd be performing exorcisms in my spare time, no one was fazed. In fact, a lot of them begged to be first in line. I decided right away that if Spirit had told me that helping people was my life's calling, I shouldn't charge any fees. That way, no one felt they had anything to lose.

Except, of course, their entities.

I was flying blind at first. The only experience I had to go on was the clumsy exorcism I'd performed on my boyfriend— which, in the end, *had* worked well—so I figured I'd go from there. Something about doing an exorcism in a different room hadn't felt right, though, so I decided to set up shop in a special place that was 100 percent devoted to my new spiritual work. I also realized that I needed to make my Spirit Room so special and specific to my intention that people would have to come to me—unless traveling was a massive, life-or-death issue.

I did my first "real" exorcism when I was thirty-one, and I'm thirty-eight now. For almost six years, until NPR aired a story about me, I only advertised through word of mouth, but, trust me, it was all the PR I needed because right away people began talking. When I first started up, I averaged one to two exorcisms a week. As the years passed, I worked up to one to two a day. Now, I have a waiting list. The majority—probably 60 percent or more—of my clients are people you would recognize. They aren't necessarily celebrities—some are high-profile managers, agents, or studio heads, whose names you see in *Variety*—but others are household names: famous politicians, actors, or musicians. I won't name those folks in this book, unless they've given me permission. Having an entity—and then wanting to do something about it—is a deeply personal thing, and my number one goal besides helping my clients is protecting their privacy.

The process I follow and the little things I do during exorcisms have evolved over time, but through each and every one— and I've done thousands at this point—I've honed my skills. I can now remove most entities within thirty minutes to an hour, in fact. I'll go into the nitty-gritty of what happens during an exorcism and provide a few testimonials from clients who have become friends, but all you need to know now is that you can believe what you read in this book. Why? Because I speak the truth about what I've seen and what I do. I also know that I am good at my job. Never, not once, have I been unsuccessful in removing an entity from a client. I have the battle scars to prove it.

Entities vs. Demons

Before we go any further, you need to know exactly what entities are and why they target humans. Every single one of you reading this has had an entity—and most likely has one attached to you right now—and I bet you'd like to change that immediately. But if you don't understand what you're dealing with, it's hard to do something about it.

The common—and daresay crude—name for an entity is a demon. Sometimes I call them that because it's easier for people not in the know to understand, but the terms aren't truly interchangeable. "Demon" is malevolent, conjuring up something religious in nature and connected to Satan. It brings to mind a Hollywood-style ghoul that makes your head spin and green bile spew from your mouth. It probably has horns, red, glowing eyes, and sharp, exposed fangs. In most people's minds, demons come from the Christian version of hell, are out to destroy you, and can only be exorcised by a Catholic priest.

These kinds of demons might actually exist, for all I know. I don't claim to see every kind of otherworldly creature that floats around the Earth. The entities, as I call them, are a bit more nebulous than demons but no less sinister. They're spiritual forces that inhabit you, feeding off your very being. They thrive on your energy, and their goal is to continue doing so as long as possible.

I use the word "attachment" when I talk about how entities interact with their hosts more often than the word "possession" simply because "possession" is a loaded word. People's perception of the term is based on what they see in movies, when a "possessed" individual's personality changes completely. An entity's effect isn't always that all-encompassing, so I don't want to give that impression. Having an entity won't necessarily make you a different person.

That said, no attachment is good, and some people walk around for decades—or their entire lives—with the same entity (or entities) attached to them and hurting them. The damage may happen because the entity is particularly powerful, or it may occur because its host has such low frequency.

Frequency: It's Not a Channel on Your Radio

What do I mean by "frequency"? In this context, frequency is your energy signature. In simpler terms, it's how you're buzzing. When you walk into a room, meet someone, and like them immediately because they radiate something positive out of every pore, these people are either masters of disguise, or they're exhibiting high-frequency energy. Frequency is the mirror of your emotions; if you're feeling depressed, angry, shamed, or emotionally heavy in any respect, you have a low frequency. If you have a high frequency, you're likely happy and at peace, with a feeling of lightness. You are having a good day.

Most entities are attracted to and are looking for specific frequencies that match their own. Some are drawn to sadness or depression, some to fear or anxiety, some to anger, and others to many different low-resonating emotional energies. Other than the fact that it's just nice to feel good (except if you're a deeply twisted individual), keeping your frequency high helps keep entities at bay.

Everyone runs on low frequency sometimes, and that means that every single person on this planet will attract an entity during their lives. I can typically sense who is and who isn't high frequency just by looking at them. Sure, sometimes it's obvious to me because they're covered with entities, and I can see the source of attachment, which may be a dark shadow or cloud hovering over them. But having a small number of entities doesn't necessarily indicate that a person is *always* low frequency. It just means they once vibrated at a low level, may have had a trauma and attracted an entity or two, and now need to get rid of them. When I see someone walking around town with no entities, I look at them and think, *That person's pretty good right now. They're in a good space.* But that doesn't mean they're always that way.

Identifying someone as *baseline* high or low frequency (meaning the energy that they vibrate at the majority of the time, when things in their lives are neutral) is a little more difficult, but it's by no means impossible. I just have to spend a little time with them, or maybe more than a little, and get a sense of their energy signature. Detecting someone's energy level doesn't require gifts like mine, but I'm a little more intuitive than the average person. I can see a person's core very quickly, spotting the trauma, downloading the information about why it occurred, and visualizing their current energy all at once. Sometimes this takes seconds for me, and I can see it before a client even tells me their name.

For example, I run in the same circles as a well-known Hollywood player, whom I'll call Mr. Sunshine. For whatever reason, Mr. Sunshine and I always seem to take the same meetings, with him in the slot just before mine. He'll leave a conference room, and a few minutes later, I'll enter without ever seeing him—and then stop in my tracks.

"Who was just here?" I'll ask. "Something in this room is amazing!"

Now, everyone in Hollywood knows I'm an exorcist, so I could start chanting and drawing pentacles on the floor in black salt, and no one would think I was any weirder than they already do. Pointing out the incredible energy in a room is tame as far as most expect from me.

"It was Mr. Sunshine," they answer. "He just left."

This man's energy is unmistakable. He's so high frequency that when I come into the space he's just vacated, I feel like he's left a beautifully packaged energy gift for me, right there on the boardroom table. Being in his presence is another matter entirely; it's like breathing clean, pure oxygen, or walking into a room at a spa whose air has been infused with Himalayan sea salt. (By the way, if you haven't been in a salt room, *run, don't walk,* to a spa that has one. Himalayan salt cleanses and purifies both body and spirit, helping you raise your frequency till you're positively buzzing.)

High-frequency energy feels like diving into the most beautiful, fresh, crystal-clear water in the world. It makes the air so clean that you just want to rip off all your clothes and bathe your naked skin in it. Honestly, I'd put Mr. Sunshine on retainer if he'd promise to wake me up every morning.

One interesting thing I've discovered is that people's personalities don't necessarily match their frequencies. I've met total assholes who are high frequency 99 percent of the time, and some of the sweetest people on earth are chronically low frequency. Someone's frequency is often tied to your perception of them, too. For instance, a low-frequency person may feel that way to you because they're just not your cup of tea, or perhaps they're just guarded. I've noticed that very abrupt people, for example, relax a little bit the more they're around you, and then your perception of their frequency can shift.

There are also people that I call "energetically sensitive," which means that they easily pick up the moods or energies of those around them. A subtle shift in energy—whether from a situation or another individual—makes them *feel* something more than others. These people include empaths, or those who suffer from social anxiety. When an entity tries to attach to them, they may actually sense it just outside their body or trying to burrow inside. No, they won't feel like they're being bitten or drilled into; instead, they may suddenly become nauseated, or they might think, *I don't know what just happened, but something is totally off.* In fact, they're sensing how an entity has latched on to their frequency.

I've gotten to a point where I can change my frequency so suddenly and dramatically that it's actually perceptible to the people around me. They won't feel it instinctively, though. I have to coach them. Here are the steps I lead them through:

I'll pick an object that I know has high-frequency energy in it. Often this is a small, round stone, which feels soothing and cool as it sits in the palm of your hand. I use these stones in exorcisms, and people always respond to them positively. I'll then ask my friend or client to hold the stone, saying, "Think about how you feel, and register that sensation. Now, put it down and consider how you feel with it not there."

They'll always pick up a subtle energy shift. It's not because the stone is making them feel a certain way; it's because the sensation of absence is cold and dark. It's blank, unlike the rock, which held a certain mass to it that was pure energy.

Next, I'll ask my client to hold my hands and sense my energy. "How does that feel?"

"Good," they always reply.

And then suddenly, I'll force a shift to a dark energy and ask them if they noticed.

"Yes!" they'll answer. "It's how I felt after I put down the stone!"

They've just experienced the difference between high and low frequency, which is the contrast between lightness and darkness. When you're out in the world, notice this sensation pass through you. If you're feeling great but then suddenly become anxious or afraid, know that that's not necessarily a change in your own frequency. You may, in fact, be picking up the energy of something else, and it could be an entity.

What Entities Look Like

There are hundreds of types of entities, some of which I'll describe in great detail. But, for our current purposes all you need to know is that while no two look alike, most are unmistakably gray or dark, and they're almost always slightly—if not entirely—translucent. They can be big or small, have human or animal features, or just look like creepy-crawly masses. Some are kind of cute (totally weird to say, but true), but those are definitely in the minority. Almost all are frightening, which shouldn't be surprising.

In an exorcism, I force an entity out of a person's body using a tremendous amount of high-frequency energy. Before I begin, I see the entity in whatever form it's held throughout its existence. That is, it doesn't change its shape or color just because it knows I'm trying to remove it. But when I start an exorcism, an entity doesn't maintain its form. Everything about it turns to pure energy, and it dissipates into what looks like smoke. Finally, at the point of the entity's demise—when I successfully destroy it right in front of my satisfied face—it becomes pure, ashen gray, like smoke from a fire.

The more time an exorcism takes, the longer an entity will keep its form. But I've never seen one that's able to withstand an exorcism and maintain shape. It may take hours to expel and destroy—recently I had one exorcism that lasted three hours—or it may happen almost immediately, but all entities blast into oblivion after I'm done with them.

Just because I understand what entities are and what to do with them doesn't mean they've decided to stop harassing me. I witness them attached to people in public spaces; I see them floating through the air, unattached but looking for their next victim; and I watch them in the process of embedding into people. And they visit me personally, though they typically do it in one of two ways. The first is the "Hey, I'm an entity, here I am!" visit, which happens when an entity approaches me with a stare-down, yet doesn't try to attach itself to me. The second occurs when an entity attempts to push itself inside me. My sense is that they do this to suss out what I am, and how and why I'm so different from most humans walking the streets. Now, I can't prove this—entities don't often speak to me—but that's the strong feeling I get. And I've learned over these years that I should trust my instincts.

These days, I'm very much in tune with how entities operate, and therefore I can completely shut out those who actually *do* try to attach to me. I don't deal with them the way I did when I was a kid, though; that was a naïve denial of my incredibly confusing reality. Instead, I work to push them out, and I do whatever I can to raise my frequency so that I'm more powerful than any entity. Sometimes all I have to say is "Get the fuck out. Get the fuck away from me!" And you know what? It works. I've raised my vibration quickly by stepping into my power.

Entities tend to shy away from groups of people because there's too much high energy in one space. That's not the case when someone's alone, though. Think about it; how many times have you felt depressed, thought to yourself, *You know, I just need to get out of the house and go to [insert church, library, bar, park, gym, or anywhere where there are lots of people and where you enjoy going]?* You usually start to feel a little better surrounded by others, right? Your frequency is higher in groups. Entities know this. But there are times when entities will attach in crowded places. I think it's because the person they've targeted is in a particularly low-frequency place personally, so they're vulnerable.

Or if you're me, it's because the entities are trying really, really hard to prove themselves.

Recently, I had a visitation like that in a crowded gym, of all places.

I'm kind of obsessive about some things, and one of them is that I like to go Spinning at least five times a week. You heard that right—I go to class every single weekday morning and maybe once on the weekends, bright and early. Those of you who Spin regularly know that sometimes you're just drawn to one particular bike for whatever reason. You may like the location in the room; you may—weirdly—have a penchant for bikes with ripped seats; or you may just be a creature of habit. I always choose the same bike. It's my bike (even if I don't own it) and I Spin better when I'm using it.

A few years ago, I encountered another chick who, like me, attended Spin class obsessively and always chose the same bike: the one directly in front of mine.

This woman wasn't even blocking my view of the instructor, but for no reason in particular, she really irritated me. We never spoke, and she seemed nice enough, but there was just something about her that rubbed me the wrong way. Each morning, I tried to ignore my feelings toward her and focus on getting a good workout, but I couldn't stop thinking, *This chick is driving me fucking crazy.*

After two weeks of staring daggers into her back, I was at a loss for what this poor girl could have done to make me so angry. She'd even smiled at me once in the locker room, which of course I found incredibly annoying. But then, as I sat on my bike one morning and pedaled away during a particularly hard ride, I saw something.

While the unsuspecting woman looked forward and pumped her legs up and down, an entity pulled itself away from the back of her head while still partially attached, turned, and looked directly at me. It was a male Wraith, skeletal, with dark, hollow eyes, staring me down and daring me to respond.

Okay, now it all makes sense, I thought. *That's why I never liked that girl.*

I'll never know what exactly the Wraith wanted to prove to me, though I suspect it was just trying to assert its place. Just like me on my precious bike, it wasn't going anywhere, and it wanted me to know that. I didn't do anything to it or say a word to the woman, though. I can't just go up to people randomly and tell them they're possessed. It's not something that's going to give them great joy to hear, and I don't feel it's my place.

What Entities Do

No entities—except the highest order (and most malevolent) ones like Realm Walkers—are out to kill you. If they did, they wouldn't be able to feed off you anymore, so the entire point of their existence would be null and void. The only time an entity *could* kill you—and it would be indirectly—is if it saps your energy so completely that you commit suicide out of desperation. There's also an extremely small chance that a person could have a very high-level entity who's feeding off so many people at the same time that murdering one of them is no big deal. I've never seen this happen, but hypothetically, it could.

Even if entities don't kill you, they can cause physical problems that range from mildly irritating to downright debilitating. In fact, a lot of people who come to me do so because they've heard I can help cure their illnesses, alleviate their symptoms, or undo the damage caused by a sickness. What they may not realize, though, is that their issues stem partly from another problem: the entities attached to them.

My clients' most common physical complaints include arthritis, headaches, nausea and other gastrointestinal issues, or infertility. But I also see clients with major life-threatening illnesses like cancer or AIDS. I may not be able to save these people's lives, but every single time, removing their entity helps lessen their pain and suffering. Why? Because not every physical sickness is *just* physical. There are many energetic reasons why people manifest physical symptoms of things. I'm not sure why, but joint pain is probably the most common issue entities cause, and typically, my clients will have visited a doctor to alleviate their symptoms, only to be given a prescription for pills that help for a short time but never fully cure them. The reason modern medicine doesn't, of course, is that the problem is entirely linked to entities.

It Starts with Trauma

It's not that the entity actually *causes* a person physical harm in all cases. Some physical issues are genetic, congenital, or purely random. But often, an entity carries the original trauma that's the source of a physical problem. I'll get into this more later, but think of it this way: When we have pain and trauma, it lowers our energy level. When that happens, we pull entities in (because they feed off of low energy), and we push the scars from our trauma down. When you feel anxiety, for example, you stuff pain and tension down deep into your body, shoving it so far away that it causes stomach pain, indigestion, or acid reflux. A terrible tragedy that shakes you to your solar plexus may burrow into the fiber of your being permanently—including your joints and your bones—causing you to become stiff, sore, and achy.

Traumas don't just produce physical symptoms; people re-act emotionally and spiritually as well. When someone suffers a personal setback, like losing a job or a loved one, they typically feel sad, vulnerable, betrayed, or intensely lonely. These are low-frequency emotions, and they block the flow of positive energy. When that happens, the trauma sits in the body, and entities flock to it. These entities may be the type with tubes extending from their bodies, burrowing deep within your heart, brain, or, most commonly, core, or have tentacles that pierce through flesh to go deep into a person's being. Others simply hover, and some don't show how they're physically attached. Or, like the one I saw on my boyfriend, an entity may simply tunnel inside a body to find a place to feed. I may not even be able to see how it's attached; I can just tell that it's there.

Trauma can sit in the body for years, and may eventually end your life. Just look at my mother. Throughout all her years, she denied responsibility for anything that was wrong with her, her actions, or her emotions. She remained deeply, fundamentally unaccepting of the effects of the trauma deep inside of her body. I'm no doctor, so I can't say this is exactly why she developed stomach cancer, but it sure seems like a plausible connection.

After she died, she came to visit me. Now, I know what you're thinking. *You're a medium, too?* Nope. I'd never call myself one, though I do sometimes see dead people, and we'll get into that later. Just know that a few months after her death, my mother visited me in the etheric space—essentially, what most people would call a dream—and she revealed to me exactly how she had stored her trauma in her body.

It was one of the most upsetting things I've ever seen.

My mom showed herself in what appeared to be a dimly lit public bathroom, with one light flickering. It looked like a scene out of *Saw*. She started calling to me, and when I saw her in the distance, she was in a wheelchair.

"Where were you?" she asked me.

"I'm here now," I answered.

Then she fell out of her wheelchair, as if she'd been pushed, stared blankly at the wall, opened her mouth, and began vomiting black liquid.

My mom was what we in the Spirit world call "freshly dead," and she was still coming to terms with what had happened to her in life and at the point when she passed. Obviously, she wasn't at peace with her death. Her illness had been sudden, shocking, and painful, and she was still frightened. The trauma was too fresh.

Mom visited me every few days for a month after that, and at first, we couldn't speak without getting into a fight. Still, I realized that she was showing up because she thought I'd understand. And I did. I knew that she was coming to grips with the person she was and how that had led to her death, and that she couldn't pass back to Spirit until she'd gone through this process. Mom hadn't accepted me when she was alive, but when she was dead, she began to.

It took about six months, but eventually Mom began to seem better, more resigned to her life and death, and we stopped fighting. In fact, she stopped visiting me because she realized she could cope with herself and her trauma on her own. There are many realms to the afterlife, and I don't believe she's passed through all of them yet, but I know she's moving forward.

The good news, though, is that traumatic situations—and their spiritual, emotional, and physical repercussions—can absolutely be dealt with while you're alive. In fact, they should be! And I can help.

I have lots of clients who come to me struggling with infertility. One woman I saw had been trying to become pregnant for several years. She'd gone through rounds of IVF, all of which were failures. Each of them had sapped her and her husband emotionally and financially, and their marriage was struggling, with no light at the end of the tunnel. The woman's doctor had sat her down recently and leveled with her.

"I'm so sorry," he said, "but I've been doing this for twenty years, and your ovaries won't produce the eggs that will allow you to conceive a baby."

This woman was in her early thirties, and she was desperate to have a child. She refused to give up and wouldn't accept what the doctor had told her as gospel. So with no medical options left, she sought my help.

"I realize there's probably no chance, but I need someone other than my doctor to tell me that I can't have a child," she said. "I just need a second opinion so I can stop hoping. It's the hope that's killing me."

After working with so many infertile women, I know that often the reason they can't get pregnant isn't physical. If a doctor can't find a biological cause and names the issue "unexplained infertility," as one had with my client, I almost always conclude that the real reason is spiritual. How do I know this? Because I can see the site of trauma in the body, and it doesn't look physical at all.

When this woman lay on her back on a bed in my Spirit Room, I peered into her body, and I could see where her blocks were right away. What looked like black smoke hovered over her ovaries. This darkness held her entities—a Wraith and a Clive— who were stifling so much energy flowing in and out of her ovaries that they'd shut both of them down. Immediately, it was clear that one was beyond repair. But on the other one, I could see the image of a baby.

"I want to come in," the child whispered to me.

I knew at that moment my client was going to become a mother.

For the next hour, I cleared the darkness and the entities out of her body, essentially performing a psychic surgery. When I was done, I turned to her and reassured her.

"I believe there is a chance," I said. "There's one ovary that's working, and there's one that's not. Keep trying. Don't give up, because I can see that there's a baby trying to come in."

I know you're probably biting your nails to hear what happened, but first things first! Let me explain what was going on in this woman's life and how a spiritual block brought in entities who affected her physically.

Most of the time, an entity that's standing in the way of conception is feeding off a trauma stemming from a woman's relationship with her mother. If you have unfinished issues with your mom, there's a latent fear in you that you'll be a bad mother, too. I can say this with confidence because I had a terrible mother, and I'm hyperaware of how it's affected me. Because my mother was so unfit to parent, I, like many others, am convinced that I'll follow in her footsteps with my own children—if I ever have them. Which I may at some point. Maybe.

From a very early age, my client had a dysfunctional relationship with her own mom, who was a mentally abusive alcoholic. After the exorcism, though, she began to think through her family issues. Her attitudes toward her mother softened, as did her anger. She started to let the past go.

Two months after her exorcism, she called me.

"I'm pregnant," she said, "and I can't thank you enough."

Happy endings like this are why I do what I do. It's why I forced myself to explore entities in all their horrific, gory detail, learned how they differ from each other, mapped out their many levels of malevolence, and mastered how to exorcise them out of you—forever.

CHAPTER 4

The Most Common Entities

I've seen tens of thousands of entities over the years, probably hundreds of thousands more realistically. Some were totally unique, and I've never witnessed anything like them again. Others were common types that appeared over and over, and still do, hovering near me without fanfare and present in almost every exorcism I do. Some entities never interact with humans; they seem content to just exist outside the realm of Spirit. Still others will do whatever they can to get our attention.

Then, there are entities that are truly blood-curdling. They have the potential to destroy the world as we know it. And unfortunately, I've come face-to-face with them, too.

But we'll talk about those later. First things first.

When I was in my early thirties and finally faced the reality that I was born to be an exorcist, I decided to organize my thinking. This wasn't a sophisticated or formal process. I didn't consult any spiritual gurus, nor did I sketch or write down what the entities I saw looked like. I just knew them intimately, recognized a pattern, and decided to make sense of it.

I realized that the entities I'd been seeing for so many years fell into a few distinct categories. Some entities felt more malevolent than others, and some I rarely saw, but it was clear that the ones I encountered most frequently fell into five separate groups.

What was also apparent to me was that each of these groups needed a name. After all, if I was going to talk to my clients about these terrible creatures that had invaded their bodies, sucking away their energy to the point that they'd become depressed, angry, or even suicidal, I had to make the beings come alive in some way. My clients needed something tangible to hang on to when we discussed what was plaguing them. If a person in my Spirit Room—who is probably scared half out of their mind—could say, "Oh, I have this thing that's actually called X, and other people have it, too!" I knew they'd feel less crazy. It's no different than when you're sick, and you've spent days walking around feeling terrible and wondering what's wrong with you. When you find out that what you have is just garden-variety bronchitis or a sinus infection, suddenly you feel like you have a better handle on both being sick and getting well.

I've named each entity according to what makes sense to me and based on how the entity looks, feels, and acts. My clients might laugh when I tell them they have a Clive—so named because these entities remind me of a Clive Barker drawing—but there's nothing funny about them. Quite the opposite; these entities are almost always dangerous.

The Diamond Chart

After I named the major entities, it made sense to list them in the order of how malevolent they are. My clients sometimes struggle to visualize what's actually happening to them—I mean, finding out you've got something called a "Wraith" can be hard to wrap your brain around—so I created a visual aid shaped like a cut diamond. I named it "The Diamond Chart," and it ranks the entities from lowest frequency (and therefore most dangerous)

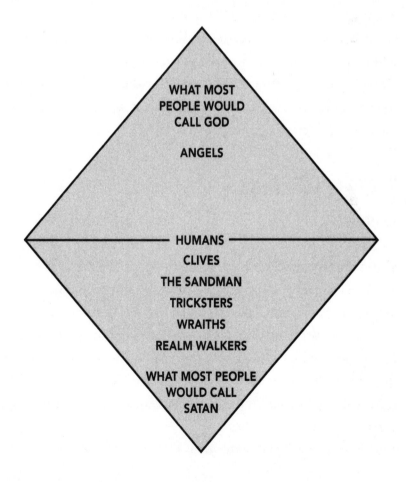

to highest frequency (and therefore most benign). The dividing line is humans, who are a mixed bag of low and high frequency, ranging between them all the time. We're rarely ever so low that we'd be on par with entities, and we're seldom ever so high that we'd be close to Higher Beings. Humans struggle with maintaining a steady frequency, so our "baseline" energy is somewhere in between.

An entity's placement on the chart doesn't necessarily correlate with how often I see them. Just because Wraiths appear toward the bottom doesn't mean I encounter them any less frequently than Tricksters. I will say that I most regularly confront Clives and least often see Realm Walkers. This is a blessing, as Realm Walkers are the most dangerous entities there are.

What follows is the Rachel Stavis taxonomy of entities: the forces I have come to know intimately, act as my constant tormentors, and serve as my life's purpose.

The Five Major Entities

CLIVES

Clives are the smallest, least harmful entities out there, and each and every one of you has had one attached to you at one time or another in your life. Clives are much like leeches; they attach to you in an effort to suck as much of your energy as possible, and lower your frequency bit by bit over time. Clives seek out a frequency that matches their own; if you're typically a sad person, that type of Clive will find you, and if you have issues with anger, you'll attract another type.

I haven't counted up how many different types of Clives exist in the world right now, but I know that there are many. Why? Because there are so many low-frequency emotions in the world, and because I see new Clives almost every week.

Clives are incredibly sneaky in the ways they attach to you, and most people will never be aware they have them, even though they might carry them around for thirty, forty, even fifty years. Clives are essentially invisible to their host simply because they amplify their preexisting negative emotions rather than create new ones. When they attach, you become the proverbial frog in hot water. If you tend toward sadness, they may cause you to enter a full-blown depression. If you have a propensity to drink too much at times, a Clive may lead you to alcoholism. If you're prone to outbursts of anger, you might become violent. Amplification is the Clive's end goal because the more you're "puffed up," the bigger the energetic frequency you release. In turn, the more they can feed.

I work with Clives constantly, and as far as I can tell, they're not sophisticated thinkers. They simply exist, just doing what they're doing and trying to prevent you from noticing them. A Clive generally isn't all that dangerous, but they can cause their host to do something dangerous. For example, if you're sad, attract a Clive, and then become depressed, the Clive may continue feeding, making you more and more desperate until you're suicidal.

I know this because I can see Clives in photographs of deeply self-destructive people. I've had clients come to me, terribly upset that someone they were close to committed suicide, and they'll ask me why it happened.

"I just don't understand," they'll say. "I knew my friend had problems, but I didn't think they were *that* bad."

"Can I see a photograph of your friend?" I'll ask.

When they show me one, the image of the Clive is unmistakable, and I know that it amplified whatever trauma that individual had faced until the pain was unbearable. Unfortunately, since they're now gone, I can't help that person anymore, but I can be there for their surviving loved one. I may perform the best exorcism I can to help them relieve their trauma, and then I might refer them to a medium to help them be in touch with the deceased—if that's what they want.

Despite the fact that Clives may help lead people to suicide, the entity doesn't have blood on its hands, if that makes sense. In fact, a Clive's goal is *not* to kill you because, if you're dead, they can no longer feed. Again, their effect is amplification of an existing trauma, and, unfortunately, that can have lethal consequences.

As I mentioned, I named Clives after acclaimed horror writer Clive Barker because they resemble some of his drawings—simple at first, but more and more creepy the longer you look at them. You can take a look online; I promise that when you do, you'll understand. Clives tend to rest in a person's core, with tubes and talons coming out of them that connect to the heart, the brain, the backs of the eyes, or the internal organs. They then feed through those tubes just like a parasite. Most are pretty tiny—even small enough to fit in the palm of my hand. But the larger ones I've seen are the size of a small dog. Clives can live in the body with other entities, which was the case with the little girl I described in the introduction. She had one very malevolent entity called a Trickster that was the source of most of her symptoms, but the Clive she also had was amplifying all of her terrible, negative emotions. Essentially, the Clive had become a megaphone for the larger entity, and that made for a dangerous, self-destructive situation for this innocent child.

Even though everyone carries Clives—or, at least, has at some point in their life—I've discovered that they frequently attach to porn stars. I have many clients who work in porn. The Valley is the hub of American adult film production, and for years I lived and worked there, so in that network, word got out about me.

Unfortunately, a lot of pornography has undertones of violence. Sure, what you see on the screen is fictionalized, and the violence may not be straightforward, but themes of domination and subversion are common. Many porn stars have had difficult pasts, too. They attract entities at an early age because of their troubled upbringings, and when they begin to work in an industry where things can veer to an intense intimacy with shades of violence, they collect Clives. Guess where these Clives attach? Their genitals. These actors may be possessed by other, more malevolent entities like Wraiths, who are typically connected to sexual trauma, but 99 percent of the time Clives are the most prevalent entity. They attach the most easily, and they do it the most quickly.

I hesitate to make any blanket statements about the porn industry here. Violence isn't necessarily the norm, and sometimes, the actors are people who approach their work as business, from a place of power and not because of their childhood demons. There are amazing creatives who do that work who have branded themselves, and who strive for body positivity and the betterment of women. But sometimes, things aren't that way. That is just fact.

I've cleaned out porn stars who then decided to leave the industry, and I've also had others who stay in it, telling me, "This is my calling." I exist in a no-judgment zone, and I believe that whatever makes you happy and doesn't hurt another person is what you should be doing. Hands down, no questions asked. I just exist to rid them of their unwanted spiritual baggage, so to speak.

While all exorcisms are similar in the steps I have to take, removing a Clive is by far the easiest for me. I call them my "pizza delivery exorcisms" because, nine times out of ten, they take thirty minutes or less. It's like removing a tick; you just pull it right off. Sure, to my clients Clives may feel huge, but they're pretenders, like cats. When a cat wants you to be scared of him, he puffs up and he hisses, but he usually doesn't lunge at you. Neither do Clives. With my prompting, they just flow right out of the body, then hover before they dissipate into a cloud of smoke.

Clive exorcisms are straightforward even when someone is covered in them, and that often happens when a person has multiple sexual partners. I've already talked about my porn star clients, but I'll describe another memorable case to illustrate this.

I once met with a character actor named George. George had never really hit it big in Hollywood, but he'd had steady jobs in television and movies for years. He was in his late thirties, was very good looking, and had bounced from set to set, all over the world, since his early twenties. I'm not sure if being on the road so much had prevented him from settling down, but he hadn't had a monogamous relationship in years, and he'd slept with probably six hundred women. Genital hopping was his thing, and he had always had several partners at once.

An individual who treats sex like a handshake probably has a lower frequency than most. I'm not judging—there is nothing wrong with an active sex life—but the truth is that a person who's focused on getting laid more than having a relationship is dealing with base-level ego rather than high-mindedness. Ego is low frequency, and that causes entities to flock to you. In addition, sex involves an energy exchange. If your partner is low frequency, and so are you, the encounter can lower your frequency even more. Couple that with the aftermath of a sexual encounter that was hollow and meaningless, and you dip even lower. All of that explains why George was positively coated in Clives.

George felt depressed for reasons he couldn't really explain, and a director he worked with suggested he visit me since therapy didn't seem to be helping.

"I've got a great, steady career and a terrific sex life. Why do I feel so bad?" he asked.

When I told him to lie down on the bed in my Spirit Room, I could see a cluster of Clives—probably fifteen in all—resting in his midsection. Their tubes and talons reached out from his core and extended toward his genitals, and while I didn't ask him to take off his pants, it was obvious where they were sucking his low-frequency energy from. I called in a few Higher Beings, lit some incense and burned some herbs, and within a half hour, the Clives were gone.

George felt *immediately* better.

WRAITHS

The next most common entity I see are Wraiths.

Wraiths are attracted to sexual dysfunction, so they attach because of any sort of sexual trauma that occurs in a person's life, whether it was in childhood, before the person was fully aware what was happening, or well into adulthood. The trauma can be straightforward, like a rape, or it can be more complex. For example, if a gay man hides his sexuality for years because his family is religious and wouldn't approve, he may attract a Wraith. All that matters is that there's a certain darkness around sexuality in general, or connected to one powerful, scarring incident.

Pornography addiction can also attract a Wraith. I'm not here to tell you to stop watching pornography if that's your thing, but I know what I see, and I have witnessed Wraiths attached to people who go too far. If you spend too much time online, away from your family and real-life relationships, if you confuse what you see on a computer with reality, or if you simply can't be satisfied in a sexual relationship because it's not like the images you watch, this creates a problem. There needs to be a steady balance between real-life and cyber sexuality for a Wraith to stay away.

Entities also tend to work through technology, so when a person spends an unhealthy, obsessive amount of time on their computer or mobile device, a Wraith may use them as portals. This happens because, for whatever reason, electronics carry a certain level of energy. A computer that's absolutely filled with pornographic downloads or Web searches will be low frequency, and if a Wraith is on the prowl, he'll know he can wait there. His next victim will be logging on soon.

Not everyone who's experienced a sexual trauma will attract a Wraith. The majority do, but I've had clients who were so high frequency, with such a positive outlook on life, that even though they'd found themselves in horrifying situations having to do with sex, Wraiths didn't attach. Some people are just made of tough stuff.

Wraiths are always attracted to the opposite sex, so men carry female Wraiths, and women carry male Wraiths. I don't know why this is, but with every Wraith I've witnessed, this has been the case, no matter what your sexual orientation is. So even if a man is drawn to other men, he'll attract female Wraiths.

Wraiths look very human, but in a terrifying, gruesome way, with skeletal arms and legs. They're always grotesquely tall and thin, as if they're anorexic. Female Wraiths have Cleopatra-style haircuts, while the males tend to be bald. Both sexes' faces are very gaunt, with dark holes in the place of their eyes and mouths. Maybe it's because they're insecure, and trying to appear bigger than they are, but the males wear cloaks or trench coats that surround them like a black cloud, hiding the lack of hair on their heads.

The closest depiction of a Wraith I've ever seen is the original cover illustration on the book *Scary Stories to Tell in the Dark*, published by Harper & Row in 1981, which was so frightening that the illustrator wasn't hired to draw the cover for the reprints. I dare you to google the original image; it's completely horrifying. Bear in mind that whenever I'm visited by a Wraith, this is very close to what I see. Now you understand why I was so terrified most of my childhood.

Wraiths appear during night terrors. Many people report that when they're having a night terror, feeling trapped in their own bodies, sometimes unable to breathe, they see black figures near them. They're lost between sleep and wakefulness, and witness a person across the room, watching or quietly approaching them. Or, they may feel something on their chest, like they're being pinned down. That's a Wraith, and it's causing a weak paralysis within the body. Wraiths never want to be hidden, and when they show themselves, they do so when you're at your most helpless.

I'm sometimes asked whether having a night terror automatically means you have a Wraith. It does not. Entities may visit you in the night and cause you to stop breathing or moving, but that doesn't indicate they've attached to you. Oftentimes people with heightened psychic awareness will have night terrors, but again, that doesn't necessarily signify that a Wraith—or any other entity—is feeding off them. The first reason may be because that person is sleeping next to someone who has the attachment, and they're sensitive to their energy. The second reason may simply be because entities are curious about highly psychic people. I really don't know why, but they're just drawn to them.

I have nighttime visitations all the time, and one of the most terrifying involved a Wraith. A few years ago, my then boyfriend and I were sound asleep. At around 4 A.M. I suddenly woke up. As my eyes shot open, I saw my boyfriend on his side, facing me, oblivious to whatever it was that had jolted me awake. For a split second I was totally confused, until I looked past him and witnessed a huge, skeletal arm and leg extend over his body. Whatever I was seeing was thin and gangly—almost spiderlike—and it was moving so slowly that I was sure it was trying to avoid my notice. I knew what it was, though. It was a female Wraith, and as her face rose up, I noticed her dark, sunken features, and her hollow, haunted eyes. She looked at me, suddenly aware that I'd seen her, and paused for a moment. *She doesn't want to hurt him*, I realized. *She just wants to show herself to me.* Sure enough, seconds later, she backed down just as slowly as she'd come, and I fell back into a restless sleep.

Getting visitations like this is very common for me. Entities are extremely curious about me, and they've tried to attach to me many times but can't. I don't allow it, of course. So instead they do what they can do: watch, attempt attachments, or simply reveal themselves. Whether they're showing off because of ego or curiosity, I can't say.

When Wraiths *do* attach, they wreak havoc. They hook themselves into a person at the base of the brain, at the front of the brain, or deep into the belly region, or core. The attachment is deep, and I always find them much more exhausting to remove than Clives. Unlike Clives, a person can only have one Wraith at a time because the entity doesn't want to compete with anything like itself. A person might have a different kind of entity with a Wraith—like a Clive, which is amplifying the symptoms the Wraith creates—but they'll never have two Wraiths.

Female Wraiths often lie in bed with the men they've attached to and then control them during sexual encounters. No, I don't know this because I've slept with these guys (not for their lack of trying, though! I'm just kidding). Instead, Spirit revealed to me what was happening in the bedrooms of some of my male clients, and I've confirmed it with them. They've agreed that they often felt something dark and heavy with them during intimate situations, and they've suddenly become angry or felt violent because of it.

That's why Wraiths have caused a lot of my male clients to become out-and-out hostile toward women they sleep with. They turn angry and chauvinistic, and then blame these women for the negative things in their lives after they've kicked them out of bed.

While female Wraiths are insidious and sneaky, male Wraiths are in-your-face and dominant, so the feelings they amplify are very different. Most women with Wraiths shy away from relationships, are frightened of sex, or feel a lot of shame about their sexual encounters.

That was the case with a client I saw a few years ago. Suzanne was a successful real estate attorney making good money and a name for herself in a competitive business. Suzanne was also deeply miserable. She'd grown up in the foster care system, bouncing from home to home, and in more than one of them, she'd been molested. She started having night terrors when she was a child and as an adult couldn't sleep without lights on. She was wary of sex *and* having a real relationship with a man. She desperately wanted to be a mother, though, and she didn't want to do it alone. She wanted her baby to have a father, yet she was terrified to find a partner.

When Suzanne came to see me, I could tell right away what was causing her fear. I talked to her, and she told me all about her troubled life. Then I asked her to lie down so I could begin her exorcism.

Since I could sense its incredibly dark energy, I knew the Wraith she had was going to be one of the most malignant I'd ever seen. So I pulled together some of my more potent blends and began to burn them one by one. Some of these are poisonous—the kind of stuff I never recommend people using at home—and they include vesta powder, blue lotus, wolfsbane, and sulfur. The energy these produce is powerful; it basically body-slams entities as it tries to banish them from my Spirit Room.

Unfortunately, even as the noxious fumes from the smoke wrapped around it, the Wraith didn't want to go. He pulled himself up to his full height, which was about as big as two decent-size men, and he lifted his bald head. His eyes were sunken, with hollow, empty sockets, and his cheeks were fleshless and caved-in, but he stared at me, refusing to look away. Then he opened his mouth and let out a silent hiss.

I didn't turn away. I never do. Even though what I was gazing at was making adrenaline pulse through me, I wasn't frightened. I can't be; if I let my frequency dip even the slightest bit during an exorcism, I'll weaken my position. When that twelve-foot-tall Wraith bent his arm and extended his bony fingers toward me, I refused to flinch, and I started circling my client to let the energy flow around her.

"Oh, my God," Suzanne said suddenly. "I feel like I'm on fire."

I peered down at her body and saw the blockages shifting inside her, starting to dissipate. *This is working,* I thought. *She's sensing the negative energy changing.* This kind of sharp, sudden discomfort happens with lots of my clients whose exorcisms require a bit more energy. They might sweat profusely, or they may clasp at their necks, unable to breathe. I looked toward Suzanne's face, and she did just that, opening her mouth and screaming silently. Then she gasped as she suddenly found her breath.

Most Wraith exorcisms take an hour or so. Suzanne's extended over a few hours, and like most of my particularly difficult exorcisms, I had to end it by blending herbs that would put positive energy back into the room. I burned what I call angelic substances (because they're so light and high frequency), and Suzanne lay silently, smelling frankincense as it floated through the room.

"You can get up now," I said.

Suzanne sat up and wiped her sweat-soaked hair away from her face. "I feel different now," she said. "I feel like a weight is gone." Then she wrapped one arm around her waist and jumped out of the bed, running to the bathroom as she muttered, "Oh, God . . . I'm going to be sick."

After Suzanne came out of the bathroom, pulled herself to-gether, and said goodbye to me, I didn't hear from her for about six months. But when she finally called me, she had great news to share.

"I'm engaged, Rachel," she said. "And he wants kids as much as I do."

I feel certain that someday she'll get the family she always deserved.

Because of how painful and profound sexual trauma can be, a lot of Wraiths remain attached to a person for years and years, as was the case with Suzanne. Recently I had one client who'd had a Wraith with her for more than forty years! She'd been mo-lested as a child, and her trauma was so deep that looking into her body almost made me cry. Like I said before, though, I can't let my emotions get the best of me during an exorcism. If I do, I let my guard down, so in this case I became very maternal and nurturing. As I looked at my client's darkness and pain, left to rot for forty years, I shifted into what I'd call a high-frequency sadness, and I touched her gently.

It's going to be okay, I thought. *She's going to be better when this is over.*

I was able to remove her Wraith, and I'm so grateful I could help her.

It's often very uncomfortable for people to acknowledge and discuss the fact that they have a Wraith because sexual trauma is such a deep, personal issue. It hits at the very core of who you are. I've found this is most true with men because cultur-ally, they're assumed to be sexually strong—and never victims. When something dreadful has happened to them, like a child-hood molestation, talking about it makes them feel weak. That's not necessarily the fault of men—or even part of their nature. It's just the havoc a Wraith causes.

That said, most people with Wraiths are aware that they're carrying around a lot of negativity. They don't deny it, though they may justify it by blaming others. But when I sit down with them in my Spirit Room before an exorcism, work with their Spirit Guides to uncover their issues, then hit them with the fact that they're so miserable because of an entity, most of them are relieved. They wonder why relationships have been so awful, sex has been so twisted or tense for them, and sleep has been so fraught with night terrors. Lots of my clients have been in and out of terrible relationships, afraid of getting too close to someone for fear that they'll be hurt. When they find out that the thing that's causing their issues can be removed, they're thrilled because they can finally see the path toward a solution.

Other times, people are reluctant to let go of their Wraiths because, unconsciously, they feel like they're being protected. If you've had a terrible sexual trauma—your partner raped you, or you were repeatedly molested by a family member—you may be too fearful to get into a relationship, thinking, *I never want to get hurt like that again.*

If I sense that kind of hesitation, I always point this out to my clients. I explain to them that it is not their rational, connected-to-Spirit side making them think this. That's a Wraith, holding them back from giving themselves to someone else. It's not there to protect them. It's there to stifle them and keep them from connecting with love.

But when their Wraith is gone, most people—especially men—report that they start having the best sex of their lives. The Wraith won't come back to them, either. Another Wraith may eventually attach for one reason or another, but once the original Wraith is gone, that's it.

Wraiths are unique among all other entities because you can inherit them. It's incredibly uncommon—and in all my years as an exorcist I've only seen it a handful of times—but if a person has a deep-rooted sexual trauma or dysfunction somewhere in their lineage, a Wraith might attach to them in the womb.

Such was the case with my clients Jen and Sylvia Soska. Jen and Sylvia are identical twins who also direct and produce films under their company, Twisted Twins Productions. We met a few years ago, when Jen and Sylvia came on board to direct a movie for which I had written the screenplay.

Jen and Sylvia were raised Catholic; in fact they were the first female altar girls in western Canada, serving under a priest who happened to be an exorcist. Unsurprisingly, they immediately took an interest in my work. Not just an interest, actually; they wanted to book an exorcism right away. Like a lot of my clients, they looked back at years of their lives and realized they'd always had a dark cloud over them. They couldn't get out from under it and couldn't move ahead as much or as fast as they wanted to, and when they met me, something clicked for them.

But here's what was really interesting: they asked to have their exorcism *together*. To anyone that knows them, this shouldn't be surprising. They're together so often they might as well be one body with two heads. But they also asked because they felt such eerily similar things to each other that they knew they must share whatever trauma they'd endured.

Now, I never take two clients at the same time, but I could tell right away that Jen and Sylvia were a special case. I saw that they shared a Wraith, which they'd inherited while they were in the womb together, and there was no way I could remove it from them one at a time.

I'll let them talk about the experience—and our relationship—in their own words:

SYLVIA: The thing about Rachel is that she knows every-thing about you as soon as she looks at you. Sometimes, it's as if she's looking through you. When I first met her, all I could think was "Okay, cool, we like each other. We like the movie we'll be working on together . . . Is there something attached to me?!?!"

JEN: I've had a pretty dark, fucked-up life, and Rachel figured that out right away. While we were sitting across from each other for the first time, she kept looking over our heads. The thought running through my head was, *Fuck. I've got to find out what she's looking at.*

SYLVIA: Finally, Jen and I just asked her. Rachel re-sponded, "Yes, you've got something attached to you. To both of you, actually, but don't worry about it because whatever you have has been there for a while." I know she said that to reassure us that we weren't facing imminent death, but at the time, I was thinking, *Sorry, but that's not so comforting!*

Jen and I set up an appointment for an exorcism together because, for the very first time, Spirit had told Rachel that she could exorcise two people together. This made total sense to me because Jen and I are *so* attached. If you ever see one of us alone, something odd has happened because we are always, always together.

JEN: When we went into Rachel's Spirit Room, she

looked at me and said, "You have an entity because of this, but we don't need to talk about it." I said, "We can . . ." and then Rachel revealed our big, ugly family secret. I was shocked.

SYLVIA: It wasn't even a guess. She just flat-out told us exactly what it was. Turns out Jennifer and I had a Lineage Wraith on us because of this nasty family trauma, and we carried it on behalf of everyone we're related to. It explained why suicide and depression runs in our family.

JEN: When I was young, I had an experience with sleep paralysis that was horrible. Most people endure those things at night, but I had one in the middle of the day. I don't even think I was asleep—just all of a sudden, I couldn't move. I tried to look around, but I couldn't. Something was right over me, and when I tried to shift or scream in my head, I wasn't able to. I felt this *pressure* of something on top of me, and being a good Catholic girl, I was pleading, "Oh, Jesus, God, please help me. What is happening to me?" I thought I was getting abducted by fucking aliens or something. Syl has experienced sleep paralysis her entire life—and night terrors.

SYLVIA: Rachel exorcised us both, and it took maybe an hour and a half.

JEN: When we'd talked beforehand, Rachel had told us, "After you've done this, the way you feel now, you will never feel this way again." And until she lifted those entities off of us, I didn't even realize what she meant. I had two entities: a Clive connected to my stomach and the Wraith connected to my head.

It explained so much. Ever since I was a little girl, I'd

had these horrible, debilitating migraines. I got visual auras that caused me temporary, partial blindness. Since the exorcism, I haven't had a migraine. I haven't even had a headache. It's like all of that was just taken away.

SYLVIA: My Clive was on my throat. What's so interesting was that I always felt so muted before my exorcism, and now I can't stop myself from talking.

The Soskas and I are now great friends and still work together, and their exorcism remains one of the most interesting I've ever done. Working on two people at once isn't just highly unusual; it's tricky. I couldn't treat them like one person with one entity, touching only one of them, and then, poof! Entity gone. Instead, I had to put them on the bed together, side by side, and work on them individually. I needed to touch them and manipulate their energy separately, moving from one to the other, and that doubled the time it took to cleanse them.

It was worth it, though, because Lineage Wraiths are nothing to mess with. They've passed from family member to family member over the course of many years, attaching to the next person through the mother in utero, and there's no way to get rid of them without an exorcism.

TRICKSTERS

Tricksters are pretty much exactly as they sound: When they attach to you, they start playing little tricks and messing with your head.

Tricksters are high up on the entity food chain because they're much more intelligent than Clives or Wraiths. When they attach to a person, they make them feel safe, essentially fooling them into believing that they're not taking away from them, but instead adding to their life in some fundamental way. Think of it like this: Tricksters are like vampires. You're drawn to them because they're so sexy and alluring. They may be a little mysterious, making you feel like you're now part of a secret club you never dreamed you'd be invited to join. Now that you're in, you're protected. But here's the rub—the entity that offered the invitation is focused on one thing and one thing only: sucking the life out of you.

Because Tricksters want a positive and symbiotic relationship with their host, they generally take whatever form will make that person feel comfortable and safe. If a Trickster attaches to you when you're a child, chances are they'll show up as an imaginary friend. Unlike most imaginary friends, though, this one sticks around well into adulthood.

Surprised that some adults still have imaginary friends? Don't be. It's more common than you think. People see them in their minds or right in front of them, and they may actually speak to them. When most people grow into adults they no longer discuss these things openly, but it doesn't mean their little buddies have stopped existing. Quite the opposite; oftentimes a person will even describe that imaginary friend growing along with them.

Tricksters that appear to adults may take the form of archangels, genies, fortune-tellers, important people in your life who have passed, or anything or anyone that you have an affinity for. If you like unicorns, your Trickster might just grow a horn in the middle of its head. Unlike Clives or Wraiths, people may actually see these entities, but, again, they're okay with it. It's their friend, and they have a symbiotic relationship.

When I encounter Tricksters during an exorcism, though, I don't witness them in the form my client does. They don't look like a cute ghost or genie to me. They may project to my client whatever the person believes they are, but I see something different. I visualize what the entity actually *is* and what it's attempting to do, which is feeding. It's not protecting or helping, which is what the host believes. I see the real entity, not the disguise.

What I witness is the Trickster trying to appear human, but unable to figure out how to. Their faces constantly shift, as if they're a character you're watching on TV as your cable connection repeatedly cuts out. Their faces time out, reappear as a different face, then flicker off like a wisp of smoke.

Trust me, this looks scary as hell. It's like staring wide-eyed into a dark, gruesome Picasso painting, or a jigsaw puzzle that keeps breaking up into a million pieces. I often compare them to Edvard Munch's famous painting *The Scream,* if the character blinked on and off.

To my clients, Tricksters don't just seem innocent; they feel downright inspiring. They truly love their Tricksters, so choosing to get rid of them is a big deal. I have many clients come to me thinking they're ready and totally willing to have an exorcism, but deep down, they can't let go. That symbiosis creates an energy that's a bit more difficult to untangle, and I may be more exhausted after the exorcism. And, unfortunately, in the back of my mind I know the client might return someday. Even though I get rid of the Trickster, I realize my client might allow another to attach. To them, it will appear to be the same imaginary friend, but in fact, it's another Trickster disguising itself.

Other clients never return. For example, I exorcised one woman named Jane, whose Trickster had been with her for more than fifty years. Jane first saw the Trickster when she was a little girl, and it appeared to her as a genie, promising to grant all her wishes and make her dreams come true. I know it sounds weird, but this was an actual genie, standing in her room, and she wasn't afraid because he was so magical and friendly. As a child, Jane was innocent. No one had told her that genies weren't real. She was giddy with hope and anticipation, and she welcomed him with open arms. But over the course of many years, he fed off her until he destroyed her. Jane's life was a garbage dump of broken relationships, unemployment, and drug addiction. Yet she still looked to the genie for answers, hoping he'd make her life perfect.

"I can't keep living this way," she said to me when I told her that her little genie friend was bad news. "I just won't be able to move ahead if I have this horrible thing with me."

She was ready, and her exorcism was successful. A month later, she called me and told me she'd gotten a job, was in the beginnings of her first real adult relationship, and best of all, she'd stopped drinking and was taking steps toward a lifetime of sobriety.

As was the case with Jane, Tricksters typically get between their host and any healthy, normal relationship that person might try to form. The Trickster will separate people from friends and family, even telling them—unconsciously—that other people are dangerous. This alienation will make that individual angry, sad, and lonely, and keep them vibrating at such a low level that the Trickster can continue feeding. As the person grows older, their romantic life will suffer because they're so afraid of intimacy, and they may struggle with their jobs because they won't trust their coworkers. Like Jane, this may lead to addiction problems. Alcohol and drugs are comforting; if you're self-medicating, you never feel as lonely as you really are.

Like Clives, Tricksters are drawn to an energy signature that's similar to their own. They have their own personalities, so they always look for someone they can really get aggro with. No two Tricksters are alike or want the same things. I've had clients with all kinds of issues: subtle, underlying anxiety, deep-seated anger, malignant narcissism, or painful introversion. They were all plagued with Tricksters.

Because a Trickster is attracted to a particular energy signature, it's unlikely that one would ever hop from one person to another. Sure, two people *could* exist on exactly the same frequency, making it possible that a Trickster—or any entity—would be interested in both of them, but it's not something I've ever seen.

Most Tricksters follow people from childhood, and they attach after a particularly dark trauma—but not one that's sexually related. A child who's abused, loses a parent, or witnesses a violent act against someone they love feels so vulnerable that they may become desperate for something—*anything*—to protect them, and Tricksters flock to them because of this. The young person will then carry the entity into adulthood, with the Trickster continuing to show itself from time to time.

"It's the weirdest thing," my clients tell me, "but I sometimes see an image of a dragon, and it makes me feel good."

"You're not crazy," I'll respond, "but just know that that dragon is not your friend."

Remember my first exorcism on my boyfriend, Peter? The one with the Clive? Well, Peter's comforting ghost was actually a Trickster.

Tricksters won't cause immediate or direct harm to someone, but, like a Clive, they may amplify negative behavior and cause someone to hurt themselves. If your Trickster leads you toward addiction, for example, you may overdose. Or if you've been depressed for years, you might consider suicide. Tricksters push you to the extremes in an attempt to feed, and while I've never had a client die because of a Trickster, I know it's happened. I've looked at photos of a dead person in the newspaper or on television and immediately realized, *Their Trickster took them over the edge.* How do I know? Because I see a genie or fortune-teller right there, next to the dead person's face. Other times, the Trickster looks like a giant blackness hovering around the person.

Tricksters and Wraiths are the only entities to age. I really can't say exactly how they're born—or, for that matter, how any entities come into being—but I've seen young Tricksters who are clearly far less sophisticated and malevolent than older Tricksters.

Believe me, these old Tricksters can be incredibly dangerous. There's even an extra-high-level class of Trickster that I've witnessed with some of my most damaged clients. I call them "Ancient Tricksters" because they've been around for hundreds—if not thousands—of years. They've used more energy, fed off more people, and know more about the world, so they're far more cunning and malevolent. Ancient Tricksters have spent their entire existence looking for a very specific host that they can damage to the full extent of their powers, and often those are people who can enact real change in society. They may not be seeking world domination, but they might be influential musicians or artists, for example. Ancient Tricksters have spent all the years before that feeding on individuals who've grown old with them, then passed away, so the Trickster had no choice but to move on to their next victim. When they finally attach to the host they've spent centuries looking for, they try to enact very insidious, deep destruction in the person's life. They're not powerful enough to cause widespread, global mayhem, but they sure as hell will turn someone into a mess.

For example, a few years ago I had several musicians come to me—all separately—complaining that they could no longer create music. These were seriously talented stars who wrote complex, hard-hitting songs. They were metal guys and punks who had defined their respective genres. All of them were major influencers, and that led me to believe that their entity was particularly malignant because some high-level entities don't just want to feed off a host; they want to draw the energy of every person who's ever flocked to see them perform.

These men's careers were falling apart, and they worried they were done for if something didn't change. They each explored all the usual means of help: therapists, long vacations, and whatever version of self-care they had, like seeing a spiritual guru or doing yoga. Some took the opposite route and escaped by having a lot of sex or taking drugs.

Each of these guys revealed that, sometimes, they saw an image of Baphomet, an ancient, goat-headed idol whom the Knights Templar were accused of worshipping in the thirteenth and fourteenth centuries (and tortured and killed because of it). Now, Baphomet is often associated with music and appears in lots of the imagery surrounding heavy metal. For my musician clients, Baphomet always made them feel better.

"I can't explain it," one drummer I'll call Jake said, "but I just feel the music so much more when I think about him."

It took me a few exorcisms, but I finally figured out that the Baphomet Trickster—who wasn't Baphomet, but instead chose to "dress" like him—was a subclass of Ancient Tricksters drawn to an energy signature that shows up with musicians. It wasn't the same entity on each man—as I said, that can't happen—but it was the identical projection to all of them.

Like most Ancient Tricksters, its energy was very dark, and it was incredibly cunning and wise. It looked old and tattered, like a mummified corpse, but it was anything but frail. The malevolent energy coming off of it was *giant,* like a nuclear bomb had just dropped into my Spirit Room, blasting fire and radiation from one corner to another.

For each of my clients, I was able to remove the entity, but it wasn't easy. In fact, one exorcism took me a whopping three hours, and it taxed my body in deep ways. I was achy and sore all over, like I had the flu, and I spent the next day curled in a ball in my room with a fever. Some of my clients felt the same for days and days. But sooner rather than later, all of them were able to make music again.

I hate seeing Tricksters, and luckily, they aren't incredibly common. Ancient Tricksters even less so. For every hundred exorcisms I do, ten will be Tricksters. Now, I've seen thousands upon thousands of entities in my life, so 10 percent still accounts for a healthy number, but they aren't as common as Clives, whom I see multiple times a day.

Despite how rare they are, they're the entity who visits me at night most often. I see Ancient Tricksters more often than not, and their energy is so malevolent that you feel like you could cut it with a knife. I'm so removed from the idea of being terrified of entities that I'm not sure you could call what I feel real "Oh my God, I think I'm going to die!" terror, but these visitations do bother me.

Several years ago I was asleep next to my then husband. I woke up at around five in the morning. There was just enough light shining into the room to illuminate a young girl standing near our bed. She looked like a college coed—blond, fresh-faced, all-American. I even thought to myself, *She's kind of pretty.* She was pacing back and forth from my dresser to the elliptical we had in the room at the time, taking articles of clothing one by one out of the dresser and placing them on the machine.

When I sat up, she looked at me and pointed.

"I found out there's a ghost in that ring."

"What ring?" Then I looked down and saw the white stone on my right hand. *Of course,* I thought, *the ring my husband at the time gave me. We called in Spirit and put an intent of protection on it. This entity wants me to remove it so I'll be vulnerable to her.*

"Who are you?" I demanded, not quite loud enough to wake my husband up. Not two seconds after the words came out of my mouth, she flew over my body, looked right at my face, and tried to enter me through my chest. But she couldn't. I knew who she was, and she wasn't going to get me.

Unfortunately, many of my clients aren't as strong. A medium I work with sometimes carries one that she absolutely refuses to face. This Trickster appears to her as the Archangel Michael, and it feeds off the very volatile, angry energy the medium emits. When I confronted her and said, "Honey, that's not an angel; it's an entity," she blew up and refused to come in for an exorcism. Why? Because she's convinced that he's trying to protect her rather than hurt her.

I've had clients come in three or four times with the same

Trickster. They'll look at me and say, "Rachel, I promise you that this time I'm ready to get rid of it. I'm absolutely ready."

"Then, let's do this," I'll respond.

But because I speak to their Spirit Guides, I can usually tell if my clients are really being honest. I'll know if the circumstances of their lives have become so desperately bleak that they realize there's no other option than to say goodbye to their Trickster forever. Unfortunately, that's the case with too many people; they have to hit rock bottom before they can actually break free. They may have lived so long with this entity that they're doubtful about who they are or what the future will hold because they've never known life without it. I'm sure my friend, the medium, probably wonders, *If my guardian angel isn't Michael, who am I? Am I not special anymore?*

That's part of the reason why I can pull a Trickster off a client a hundred times, but they'll still want them to come back. A client who's ready to vanquish their Trickster for good doesn't just have to *want* them gone; they need to be at a point in their lives when they realize that their problem is caused by that entity. They need to stop making excuses, blaming their unsupportive boyfriend or mean boss, and acknowledge that the thing that's been as comforting as a baby blanket is actually bad news.

When I encounter a Trickster during an exorcism, it usually tries to fight me. This could be verbal; it might curse or try to engage me in some sort of back-and-forth argument. And yes, it actually speaks. Or it might talk through my client, causing their voice to become gravelly and low, just like you see in the movies.

The entity may engage in physical violence, too, and it's not uncommon for them to compel their host to reach toward me and grab me hard. I'm used to this, so I've never been hurt, but it's still a shock. The Trickster isn't just resisting, it's trying to inflate itself to a higher status so it can inflict actual damage on me or my client. It doesn't *ever* want to leave, and that's why the three days after an exorcism are key to preventing other Tricksters from coming back. I'm always vigilant about telling clients to ignore the little voices in their head that urge them to do harm. They *must* be extra good to themselves, never judge the up-and-down emotions they're going to feel, and above all, refuse to remember their Trickster as anything but pure evil.

SANDMAN

There are some entities that don't attach to people. They either won't stick with one person, refuse to interact with humans, or come face-to-face with many people but choose not to invade one single individual. In the next chapter I'll focus on the most dangerous free-floating entities, but for now I want to describe one that has touched almost everyone reading this book.

That entity is the Sandman, and like the song says, he'll bring you a dream. But instead of it being the cutest you've ever seen, it's always absolutely terrifying.

The Sandman looks like a shadowy figure of a man with an old-fashioned, wide-brimmed hat. He's like a supercreepy version of the Quaker Oats guy. The Sandman doesn't target one person; instead, he searches for a large area like a city block, a building, or even an entire small town. After he focuses all of his negative energy on that particular space, he wraps it with an etheric energy that looks like spiderwebbing. When his target is completely covered, he sits back, satisfied, and waits.

It's never clear how long the Sandman stays around. All I know is that after the sun goes down and people go to bed, he starts his nasty work.

When as many people as possible are asleep, usually in the middle of the night, the Sandman begins to pull energy from the heads of everyone under his web. The less energy each person has, the lower their frequency, and they begin having nightmares. These aren't your typical nightmares, though; they're endlessly long, detailed, graphic, movie-style dreams that leave you feeling spent when you wake. I know this not just because Spirit's revealed it to me, but also because of all the many stories my clients have told me—as well as my own experiences. The Sandman's visited my neighborhood a few times through the years, and I've had dreams ranging from discovering I couldn't walk, then trying for hours to pull myself up to standing, to reliving the weeklong death of my grandfather. I woke up sobbing both times.

I know many of my neighbors did, too. As we all slept under the Sandman's web, helpless, suffering through terrible, epic dreams, the Sandman lurked above and fed off our fears. Most of the time, everyone under his web will have different nightmares, but all of them will wake up exhausted after a long, restless night.

I've also witnessed the Sandman working on buildings and houses while I stood apart from him, unaffected. But, again, I don't just understand him based on my personal experience. Just like every entity, I've learned about him because I commune so deeply with Spirit.

I call entities like the Sandman wanderers. They move from location to location without attaching, so I have no methodology to remove them. The thing that makes the Sandman different from most wanderers, though, is that he isn't neutral. He doesn't just pass through a space. He uses it to target individuals and pull out a specific frequency. He wants your negative frequency, and even though he doesn't attach to you, he draws it out, energetically, from your head.

In the midst of an exorcism, never once have I encountered a Sandman, but that's not surprising. He's moved on as of sunrise. It's just part of his nature. He's simply an annoyance, an entity who creates discomfort but who is never going to do real, direct harm.

My encounters with the Sandman have been more complex than other people's, but it's probably because he knows that I'm onto him. Once, I was having an epic dream that I was pregnant and then, suddenly, lost the baby. As if that wasn't distressing enough, my house was then destroyed in a fire, and I was left with nothing. My sense of loss was deep and intimate in this dream, and I couldn't see a way to happiness again. Just when I was feeling my absolute lowest, I woke up. Jesus Christ, did I feel drained! I was more tired than when I'd gotten in bed.

I forced myself up and walked toward my bathroom. As I approached it, rubbing the sleep from my eyes, I suddenly butted up against something sticky. Pulling my face and hands back, I walked backward and hit the same filmy substance. *It's the Sandman's web,* I suddenly realized. Then I looked toward my bathroom, and I could see its shimmering silkiness reflected in the mirror and coating the walls of everything in sight.

I gazed toward my living room, and sitting there on the couch was an older man. He was wearing a wide-brimmed hat, and he was waiting patiently, as if he had all the time in the world.

I knew right away it was the Sandman. But there was nothing I could do; he'd already fed on my fear, and it was time for him to move on.

There are people who suffer from really vivid nightmares almost every night, but this is not necessarily due to the Sandman at work. The Sandman wants a very specific type of energy, and it has to be sudden, intense fear—the kind that electrifies you from your head to your toes. If you're having regular, lower-level nightmares, you're probably a little more used to your fear. You're just a tormented person, sadly, and while I can't say for sure without doing an exorcism, it's likely that you have another type of entity attached—perhaps a Wraith. The Sandman doesn't care about your slow, scared drumroll. That's just not his way.

Neutral Entities

All of the entities I've described in this chapter are negative—that is, they feed off of low energy, leading to more of it—but there are some that are completely neutral. They don't interact with people at all; they just come out of Spirit and move through space, and judging from what I see, they don't do much of anything at all.

The neutral entity I see most often is what I call the **Poof**. That's right. I gave him and all his nonthreatening bros silly names because they're as mundane as the pile of lint sitting in your dryer. These entities are just *there,* and they're never really a nuisance. The Poof is a small ball of smoke that shifts in and out, appearing and disappearing, as it moves through space. I estimate that I see a Poof a few times a month, and like I said, it never attaches to anyone.

I named another neutral entity the **Crystal Dragon** because it appears as pieces of crystal as it floats through space, usually from one side of a room to the other. Its form doesn't really have a head or a tail, though it shapes itself into an S, like a dragon kite you might see flying through the air on a windy day.

While I can't detect any level of energy from the Poof or the Crystal Dragon, the entity I call the **Furby** has a distinctive negative frequency. Even though he has cotton-candy fur, huge eyes, and a tiny mouth that makes him the cutest entity you've ever laid your eyes on, he doesn't emanate anything good. In fact, when he moves past me, I feel nauseated. Still, I've never seen the Furby attached to anyone, so I have no reason to believe he's harmful.

Given that they don't do much of anything—and unlike other entities, don't cause harm—I'm not sure what purpose these types of entities serve. I've thought a lot about this, though, and I think it's arrogant for us, as humans, to believe that *we're* the purpose of everything, or that if something doesn't affect us, it doesn't matter. In the realm of Spirit, which I strive to be a part of daily, thinking that way isn't right. Maybe the Furby and the Poof secretly support other entities, and they're so good at what they do that I'll never find out why or how. Just because *I* can't know this doesn't mean that they don't carry weight in the Spirit world. If their existence contributed nothing, they probably wouldn't exist.

I only hope they're not helping support the next two entities because, trust me, they have all the power they need.

CHAPTER 5

The Most Dangerous Entities of All

I've reserved the two most malignant entities I encounter for last. I didn't do so to save the big scare for the end. I did this because these forces are truly, deeply dangerous. They need special attention. If you encounter a Realm Walker or a Collector—which I hope to hell you never do—I want you to have all the information I can give so you might deal with them effectively. Knowledge is power—especially when you're dealing with entities as potent as these.

COLLECTORS

There are many entities who attach to structures like hotels and office buildings. Some are harmless, while others can bring down an entire floor. Most location-based entities show up so infrequently and with so little fanfare that they're not worth mentioning, nor have I given them names. And like the Poof or the Furby, I haven't figured out why they exist. But I encounter a location-based entity called a Collector fairly often, and while it's less malicious than a Realm Walker—the next entity I'll describe—it's still not to be trifled with.

Collectors attach to places that are sources of negative energy, meaning somewhere horrible events occurred in the past. You know there might be that storefront in your town where no matter what business goes into the space, it fails? Or the apartment building that always seems to be full of sad, lonely renters living by themselves? For the Collector, that's not even negative enough. It seeks out somewhere like a house where a murder occurred, or a hospital that was the site of an outbreak of a deadly disease. It typically chooses big buildings simply because people go there consistently, often en masse, and it always seeks out places where death occurred. I've taken private tours of the Winchester Mystery House in San Jose—built by the millionaire widow of the founder of Winchester Repeating Arms, and rumored to be filled with the ghosts of people killed by guns— and there's absolutely a Collector inhabiting that place. In fact, I can sense that this Collector compelled Old Mrs. Winchester to build that strange building. A mall where a mass shooting happened would also be a Collector's dream come true. Why? Because in locations where horror like this occurred, there's negative frequency written on the walls, literally, by the spirits of the dead, and the Collector wants to gather up that energy to feed off it. That's right: when this entity attaches to a space, it collects deceased spirits and hangs on to them like little souvenirs.

Like Realm Walkers, Collectors are massive—as large as whatever space to which they've become attached. I've seen them as big as two-story buildings. Most of the time, they take on the shape of the souls of the beings they've collected, so when I look closely at them, I see dead people or animals instead of their shadow. I can spot faces, arms, and legs inside them, all of which are attached to trapped souls. Think of a huge wave full of fish, shells, debris, even a shark. (Google it! There are photos of this happening!) That's what a Collector looks like. When you exorcise the entity from a space, washing away all the trapped souls in the process, all that's left is an imprint of the entity. Essentially, for just a moment, there's a lingering shadow, almost like residue, with dark smoke hovering above. Then, just as fast as a wave can rise up and crash to the shore, that dark smoke dissipates. Sometimes, Collectors are thin and muscular, almost sinewy in their build, with huge, long-fingered hands, which they use to trap souls.

Collectors aren't incredibly common. I see them much, much less than the entities people carry—like Wraiths—and I certainly encounter them less frequently than Clives. For every ten Wraiths, I see one Collector, and I rarely exorcise them. In fact, I've only done three Collector exorcisms: one on a bank building where there had been a massive, deadly fire, and another in a house where multiple murders had occurred. The third took place on a television set, and I'll describe that in a later chapter.

In each of these locations, dead souls were stuck—held captive by the Collector—and hadn't been able to pass back into Spirit. They'd experienced horrible trauma before death, then taken their last breaths strangled by panic and fear, and they were trapped in the places and frame of mind in which they'd lost their lives. This a terrible, desperate situation, and if I can't get rid of the Collector, these souls will never reenter Spirit.

Collectors don't just control deceased people. If they've taken over a building, they can overpower individuals who live or work there, causing them to say things they wouldn't normally say—and that are counterproductive or harmful to others. They can cause destructive events within the building that can lead to injuries, and they can render a place so miserable that everyone working or living there becomes unhappy.

People aren't necessarily repelled from sites where Collectors live. Sure, they may feel an awful, ugly vibe radiating in these places, but they'll still live, work, and visit there. When I've walked around the grounds where the Manson Ranch used to be, for example, I'm certain there's a Collector present, and yet thousands go there every year to experience that ugly chaos. The Collector didn't compel Charles Manson to do what he did—he surely had his own collection of personal entities—but it's no coincidence he chose to start his commune in a location where a Collector was stuck. In many ways, a Collector is a magnet, and when it traps what it can feed on, it will never let go.

Until, of course, I come in.

REALM WALKERS

Hands down, the most toxic and malevolent entity in the world is the Realm Walker. Fortunately, it's also the entity I see least frequently. If I encountered Realm Walkers in even a fraction of the exorcisms I perform, *I* wouldn't just be spent. All of humanity would be well on its way to a violent, brutal end.

When you're faced with a Realm Walker, you might as well be dealing with the Devil himself. In fact, when people attribute large negative events to Satan, chances are, Realm Walkers are the cause. Practicing Christians describe Satan as the single most powerful force of evil in the world, but I see many devils in the world—and I know them all as Realm Walkers.

From a very early age, Spirit made me aware that Realm Walkers existed. I believe Source knew what my life path would be, and that I'd come up against at least one Realm Walker in my future, so it delivered this realization in a slow, dawning manner rather than through a full-scale visual attack. I sensed a steady drumroll of extreme low frequency. Then, when I was around eleven and was emotionally ready, Spirit began to send me unvarnished images, both in my dreams and when I was awake. What I'd see in front of me was a giant, looming blackness; an all-encompassing evil, the likes of which I didn't know existed. I was terrified. I had to turn on the television in my room and keep all the lights on just to fall asleep. *What if one tries to kill me?* I'd think as I drifted off. *What if one causes the world to end?*

The sad truth is that one Realm Walker, who finds the right host and hooks into them, just might. This is not something I say lightly. But it is something I know to be true.

A Realm Walker is cunning, intelligent, and malevolent— like I said, the most lethal of all the entities that originate in Source. Its intention is to find someone or something, attach to it, and use it as a pawn to enact global destruction or manifest negative worldwide change. A Realm Walker is a movie-style demon who can descend on a building, feed off its negative energy, and then cause many injuries to happen inside. It can break gas lines, move furniture around dangerously fast, and

worst of all, influence people who live or work in that building to kill each other. If a Realm Walker attaches to a person, it
will compel that individual to use any means necessary to exert
negativity toward everyone and everything in his or her path.
Think Hitler. Visualize Charles Manson. And I'm not naming
any names, but there was a Realm Walker very present in the
2016 U.S. presidential election.

Realm Walkers are only interested in inhabiting people
powerful enough to affect major world shifts, like politicians,
business leaders, and influential celebrities. They won't seek out
an average Joe, living on a farm in Iowa, with no great aspirations
beyond feeding his cows. Realm Walkers won't *make* you hit the
global stage; that had to be your own intention. Chances are
you'll never be *directly* affected by a Realm Walker—meaning it
won't attach to you—but it's very possible you could get caught
in its path in one way or another. Stalin, for example, had a
Realm Walker, and while the entity itself didn't murder anyone,
it did influence Stalin to order the deaths of millions.

Luckily, there's no possible way that someone could have two
Realm Walkers. First off, the world would probably spontane-
ously combust if that happened, and, second of all, each Realm
Walker is so powerful that they can't exist in the same space. The
result would be like trapping two cats in a pillowcase.

When I see a Realm Walker, they're unmistakable, and their
energy is so malevolent that it nearly knocks me over. Sometimes, I catch one hovering over someone on television or in old
photographs, and it looks like a giant dark cloud or shadow. In
public appearances—say, if a movie star is accepting an award in
front of millions of television viewers—the Realm Walker won't
show its face, but it casts an unmistakable darkness.

If I come face-to-face (or even close to) a person with a Realm Walker, the entity looms physically huge, like a giant, imposing king. In fact, its mass is its most recognizable feature. It's a sudden, torrential thunderstorm that envelops the sky and changes day to night in a matter of seconds. Sometimes I compare them to Orson Welles in *Citizen Kane,* but they're far more demonic, like how you'd imagine Satan looks. They frequently arrive as tall, cloaked figures, but unlike a Wraith, who appears to be bald, tall, and skinny, Realm Walkers are physically strong, and when they're attached to individuals, they show their muscular bodies. They can change their size depending on who or what they're targeting, and as they feed, they grow even larger. This may sound strange, and I have no idea the reason, but a Realm Walker wears a huge crown made of wood—or maybe it's an entire tree given its size. Finally, Realm Walkers are definitely masculine, with long, odd-looking faces. They sometimes have beards, and when they do, they're also made of wood. I know these are incredibly detailed descriptions for something I've only seen a handful of times, but, believe me—a Realm Walker is something you just don't forget.

Realm Walkers can be attached to individuals or to locations. When I witness Realm Walkers on structures, they're larger than the building itself, like giant robots straight out of an old-fashioned disaster film, descending on a particular part of town.

The worst part of encountering this type of entity is the fear a Realm Walker strikes within me. When I see one, it's like looking into a black hole of evil. I immediately feel a complete revulsion, like my body is working against me, and I often throw up. I start sweating. I get the chills. I've never had cancer, but I imagine the pain of your cells morphing and attacking your organs is quite similar to the sensation a Realm Walker gives me. The feeling isn't all internal, either; I sense the violence and the anger all around me. Remember when you were a kid and you shuddered and turned inward when you heard your parents fight? Did you ever cry or hide because you were so afraid? Multiply that times 1,000, and that's what a Realm Walker feels like to me.

What happens after a Realm Walker attaches to someone really depends on that person's agenda. Unfortunately, that's what frightens me the most. If I see a Realm Walker, I know immediately he and his victim are up to no good, but I have no idea what they're planning, nor is there anything I can do to stop the destruction unless the host comes in for an exorcism. Together, the host and the entity, who have a deeply symbiotic relationship, could be plotting nuclear war or in the midst of toppling the banking system. They might be setting a genocide in motion, or they may be about to take over a nation in a hostile coup. All I know is that the Realm Walker's looking to set off a major tipping point in a society—and it's going to be negative.

Unfortunately, world changers who have Realm Walkers are the people who are least likely to come to me because they have a symbiotic relationship with their entity. It makes them feel powerful and driven. They can really *do* things that affect a lot of people, and that's an ego rush. But they've—quite literally—made a deal with the Devil. In exchange for great personal power, immense wealth, a phenomenal career, terrific sex, or the huge influence they've always craved, they're in fact charting a course of destruction.

Of course, to the host, death and mayhem isn't something to fret over. It is simply an unfortunate by-product of getting to be so damn influential. Someone with a Realm Walker realizes they have something helping them, lifting them up, but they don't acknowledge, nor are they even aware, that it's a malevolent force. Instead, they believe they have a God-given gift. This symbiosis is sort of similar to how a Trickster behaves, but the difference is that Tricksters attach to people who are inherently good. When they're not feeling isolated, they have the ability to vibrate at a high level. The Realm Walker, on the other hand, will never pick a positive person. They look for someone who's low frequency by default, who *likes* being that way, and who manipulates that negative power to their own ends. To attract a Realm Walker, a host needs to be petty and small; someone who wants and wants and wants.

All that narcissism doesn't come without a cost. People with Realm Walkers attached to them *will* reach rock bottom. Generally, that breaking point is a health crisis. They may lose a tremendous amount of weight, develop a life-threatening illness, or simply look so poorly that an instinct for self-preservation takes over. The insistent nagging of family and friends that they change their lives finally gets through, and the host will realize that they cannot keep living in the same way. To make a change and be exorcised is a huge step—and it can't come without a lot of support from others—but it's the only choice an infected person can make to better their lives. To *save* their lives, in fact.

Realm Walker exorcisms are exceedingly rare. In fact, I've only done a handful in my career, but they're the most difficult by far. Exorcising a building is much more difficult than getting one out of a person because in a building, there's an enormous number of spaces, rooms, nooks, and crannies that the entity has invaded over time. There's just more required of me, more negative energy to remove.

How is this different than a Collector, you ask? First off, a Realm Walker looks different. He's an evil king while a Collector is more of a dark swell. Second, the feeling I get from a Realm Walker is infinitely darker. There's a hotel in LA called the Cecil, which I'll talk about soon, and I can feel its Realm Walker from Pasadena, which is almost fifteen miles away. Finally, a Realm Walker can pull in people from all over a city or area, controlling many individuals at a time and turning them against each other. A Collector doesn't do that.

Exorcising a person with a Realm Walker is by no means easy. It is the closest I come to the kinds of exorcisms portrayed in film, full of theatrics, drama, and a great, big mess.

Unfortunately, I can't name the people who have come to me with a Realm Walker—or even describe them or their situations in exact detail—because not only would you recognize them immediately, but I worry that the idea of them having Realm Walkers would cause mass panic. Just know that even though I've always survived, I've never come out of one of these exorcisms unscathed.

I performed one such exorcism for a famous actor I'll call Mr. Bad Vibes. This man was young, handsome, and very, very angry. He'd had a terrific career right from the start, but he'd had a tremendous number of volatile relationships that flamed out quickly—and all in the tabloid eye. He had a lot of people around him, though, and when he started complaining about insomnia and began getting in fights almost every day, one of them intervened and suggested he see me. They didn't know the depth of his torment, but when he came over, as dark, negative, and brutally frightening as anyone I've ever met, I was about to find out.

"I think I'm going to murder someone," he said when he walked into my Spirit Room. "I'm not just imagining what it would be like to watch a person die, either. This isn't some fantasy. I actually want to do it."

"Do you have one person in mind?" I asked, as straightforward as I could be. I wasn't afraid. Like I said before, if I let one ounce of low frequency enter me when I'm facing an entity as malevolent as what was in front of me, my client's done for.

He looked down. "No. But I'm going to do it."

Part of me wished he'd said a name. The fact that he hadn't meant that things were worse than I feared. Someone who just has the *sense* that they might kill someone, but not a particular target, is the most dangerous because you don't know which way they'll go. They may become a serial killer. They may enter politics and help start a war. They might infect an entire town with a contagious, deadly disease.

His exorcism took three full days, and I hardly got any breaks. I knew if I rested, the entity would regroup and come up with a different plan to try to kill me and my client. Because Mr. Bad Vibes had been cracked open like a rotten egg, I couldn't let him go home once we started. It was just too dangerous. He had to spend the night in my Spirit Room, weak, tired, and disoriented.

Everything you can imagine happened during his exorcism: Chairs flew across the room, Mr. Bad Vibes vomited repeatedly, for hours on end, and bile spewed from his mouth. A rash broke out all over his body, and I watched him scratch at himself so much his skin turned raw. Every single one of his limbs and his torso convulsed, and at one point his whole midsection arched up as he threw his head back and gasped for breath. I never considered calling 911, though, because I knew if I did, the Realm Walker would sense weakness and defeat us.

My client moaned, screamed, and retched, as much from the pain the entity was inflicting as from the energy that was moving inside him like a hurricane. When the Realm Walker became tired of working so hard physically, it began an emotional assault, causing my client to speak in other languages. Then, it started telling stories about my client or me—all of which were disgusting, and none of which were true.

"You fuck everyone in town, you dirty whore," it said.

I wasn't alone in that room. I called in Hecate and the Egyptian goddesses, whom I almost always work with, as well as St. Michael and St. Germain. I called in Archangel Michael for protection for us both. They never left me, and I continuously burned my most poisonous blends to frighten the entity.

Even though I felt like I was on the front lines of war—exhausted, drenched with sweat, filthy, and beaten down—I didn't do anything differently during that exorcism than during any other. I forced the same high-frequency energy into my client to push the entity out, but I did it more, for longer. As much as I wish I had a special bag of tricks for these extradifficult exorcisms, I just did what I did and trusted in Spirit.

And it worked, just like every other exorcism. Exactly like every single time I've steeled myself and suffered through a Realm Walker exorcism, the entity didn't explode from the pressure like you'd think it might. Instead, it just disintegrated right in front of me, never to return. What a pathetic exit given the battle it just went through.

Mr. Bad Vibes left his exorcism so exhausted he thought he'd never recover. His manager made up some excuse about where he was, like he was on a long vacation or at rehab, and he wasn't seen in public for a month or so. But when he emerged, he became a very spiritual person, and he's developed an even stronger support system around himself. He started getting better roles because he was filling himself with light and good energy. All his life, he'd mistaken darkness for power, but after his exorcism he realized that darkness was only the illusion of power. He learned that unless he embraced high frequency, he could never be the agent of change he wanted to be.

I haven't spoken to him since, but I've watched him from the sidelines, and I can confidently say he's doing well. He's changed.

After the exorcism, I was, too. I slept a full three days, and when I finally pulled myself out of bed, I took a long walk in Forest Lawn Cemetery—in my opinion, the lightest, most beautiful spot in Los Angeles, full of Mary and Jesus and all kinds of happiness—and decided I wouldn't work for another month. I deserved the break. My life was better because I defeated a terrible force, and my world was richer because of it. Best of all, my client's life was richer, too.

CHAPTER 6

The Source of All Things

Source can be called many things: I usually say "Spirit," but you can also refer to it as the universe, ethereal realms, heaven, God, or whatever term holds meaning for you. Spirit is the foundation of everything we are; it's where each and every one of us comes from and where we'll return when we die. Even though negative forces, such as entities, come from one of the many layers of Source, it's still always positive because it can provide you with everything you'll ever need to live well. Answers to all of the world's questions lie there—if you know how to access them.

People sometimes ask me how I came to my understanding of Source. I honestly don't have a clear answer, but I suspect it was always part of my awareness. Because I saw entities from such an early age, a bit of me must have understood that I partially lived in the world of Spirit. And because my mind was always so connected to it, I learned how to get comfortable with it and then visualize it. Next, I taught myself to communicate with it. I actually spoke to Spirit often when I was very young, always out loud and always while I was by myself. But eventually I stopped, afraid of what others might think if they heard me.

I embraced the idea again in my twenties, and now, in my thirties, I am in regular communication with Spirit. I have to be. When I don't have an answer for something in my life, I'll turn to Spirit, and I'll get an answer. I'll sometimes ask for help finding ordinary things that I've misplaced, like my keys. Or, once, when my cat got loose in an area rife with coyotes and I was desperate after looking everywhere, I decided to stop, center myself, and ask Spirit. Just like it had so many times before, it led me right to him.

But I rely on Spirit for more important issues, too. When I'm having trouble making a decision about my career, I'll ask Spirit to guide me. I may be presented with three projects, and I'll be torn as to which to choose.

Should I do this project, or should I not? All of them have their good qualities, but I'm not sure which one is the best for me. Which one can I give the most of myself to?

Spirit doesn't always answer me directly or in a straightforward way. It doesn't whisper in my ear. As a writer, I respond to written language, and sometimes Spirit flashes words in my mind that I'll have to piece together and make sense of in order to understand the message. Other times, the answer comes in creative ways that are unique to me—and might otherwise be imperceptible if I didn't know to look for them.

For example, I keep a lot of old-fashioned black-and-white composition books around my house. Entities like to mess up technology—especially by erasing things like hard drives, saved documents, and notes on your phone—so I can't count on devices like most people can. This isn't unique to me; a lot of people experience electronic issues because of entities, but they don't realize what's actually occurring, or it doesn't happen to them very often. I'm very high frequency, though, so I experience it more than most—especially when I'm emotional and putting out more energy than normal. To get around writing on my laptop or phone, I buy composition books in bundles and use them for everything from story ideas to shopping lists. And, because I'm such a mature, level-headed adult, I also decorate my composition books with stickers. Most of the time I pick Earth or star stickers, but one month I chose dinosaurs just because they made me happy. I'm a dark gal, but I still have my moments.

Perhaps it's that adorable personal touch I give my little books (just kidding), but Spirit gravitates to them as much as I do. Sometimes, when I need guidance, I'll close my eyes and put a pen in my hand. Then I'll pick up whatever composition book feels right, open it up, make sure the pen I'm holding is actually touching the paper, and start asking Spirit questions.

Can you help me?

Sure enough, my hands will start writing on their own, moving like the planchette on which you place the tips of your fingers when you're playing Ouija. They glide effortlessly on the paper, and I don't feel like I'm exerting any pressure.

Unfortunately, what flows onto the page—over a few minutes or a few hours—is a complete mess. There might be lines on one corner of the paper, scribbles on another corner, a word standing alone on an otherwise blank page, and five straight rows of something like this: ∧∧∧∧∧∧∧∧∧∧. No one except me would *ever* be able to make anything out of this scribble, but without fail, I understand it perfectly. This automatic writing provides me the answer I was looking for each and every time. I'm not the only person who does this—it's a known spiritual practice—but I can safely say I'm the only nondenominational exorcist who does.

My automatic writing doesn't only relate to my own life. It also gives me information relevant to a client who has an upcoming appointment with me. For example, I once began writing words like "baseball" and "bat" in one of my composition books. I know next to nothing about baseball, so I thought to myself, *This sure as heck is* not *about me.*

Later that week, I performed an exorcism on a man who'd been adopted and had never met his birth parents. Unfortunately, he never would because both of them had passed. But I sensed that the words I'd received were for him, coming through Spirit from his dead biological father.

"Are you into baseball?" I asked.

"I love it. I collect signed baseballs," he answered. "I spend tens of thousands of dollars on them sometimes."

"Well, your biological father is trying to connect to you through that. He was into baseball, too."

Talking to Spirit also reassures me that I'm not alone, that in fact I'm deeply connected to something higher that's actively helping me to make the world a better place. I need to know that Source will be there for me no matter what, allowing me to rid those who seek my help of the entities that plague them. I'll communicate with Spirit and its Higher Beings about my life purpose, what to expect after a difficult change, and how to cleanse myself of old, outdated patterns. I also talk to Spirit this way at the conclusion of most of my exorcisms, when I'm feeling exhausted and raw. I need to get my strength back, and I know that for the next few days, I'm going to need Spirit's protection as I go back into the world.

I'll close my eyes, take a deep breath, and think about Source. Then, I'll say these words out loud: "This week, how will I know you're with me?"

I always hear a little voice in my head that gives me the answer. For example, once Spirit responded softly: *We'll send feathers to you.*

That week, I found feathers on the top of my car, peacock feathers on my lawn, and parrot feathers on the street. Feathers were *everywhere* for seven straight days.

How You Can Connect with Spirit: The Big Picture

After talking to Spirit every single day for almost thirty years, and doing exorcisms for the last decade, I've come to realize that we all enter this world deeply, intimately connected to Source. No one's born without a soul. In fact, we're blank slates brimming with Spirit until we start interacting with the world at large. As soon as we take our first breath, though, we put ourselves at risk. Even the smallest trauma a child might feel—such as hunger or worry that they've lost their mother in the grocery store—may push a person down, lowering their frequency and clouding their connection to Spirit. Soon enough, entities come in and obscure that relationship even more. But they're not just disrupters; entities are looking to deplete your positive, straight-out-of-Spirit energy by feeding off it.

Like all of you, I'm no stranger to trauma. My stepfather was a true father figure to me, and I lost him when I was sixteen. A few years later, my beloved grandfather, who'd suffered from diabetes for years, started to decline from complications. He finally was admitted to the hospital and was there for a week while his body became more and more septic. I visited him every single day, and I knew the whole time he was going to die very soon. The doctors were honest that he might not recover, but it was more than that; I always have a second sense when I'm with someone near death. I can tell right away which way things are going, and with my grandpa, I knew there was no way he was going to make it.

A few years after that, my grandmother, whom I loved more than anyone I've ever known, also passed away. I had lost three of my most favorite people in the world in less than ten years, at a point in my life when I hadn't fully learned to understand myself, let alone how trauma affects me, and it left me shattered. I hid from my pain, stuffing it down and trying to get over it. I didn't see a therapist, and I had terrible anxiety all the time. I drank too much and mixed booze with pills. I never touched hard drugs like heroin, and I never went to rehab, but I was definitely a dance-on-the-bar kind of girl—every single night for months.

Maybe it was because of my mom's inability to deal with anything emotional, but I'd been conditioned to fear my feelings. I believed, somehow, that experiencing pain would destroy me. If I'd communed with Spirit, I could have broken out of that illusion and developed an energetic support system. But at the time, I didn't. I wasn't just weak and low frequency; I was completely destroyed and wouldn't have seen or felt Source if it had slapped me in the face.

But I was a different person in my teens and twenties than I am now. Once I accepted the fact that I would always see entities, learned how to talk to Spirit, and used my gift for good, I realized that facing trauma head-on is mostly about how you choose to view the world at large. If you can do that bravely, with Spirit on your side, you won't suffer. Traumas just won't beat you down, at least not long-term. Instead, you'll make it through tough times with a clear head, growing and nurturing your connection to Source.

In later chapters, I'll give you specific meditations, herb blends, and additional tools that can help you remove mental blocks that encourage entities to attach. I'll also offer details about tangible, physical things you can do to raise your frequency. But first, let me teach you about the mind set I've adopted that both is hostile to entities and also promotes a deep and important connection to Spirit that protects and guides me.

Staying High While Feeling Low

In the past fifteen years, I've gone through many life changes in quick succession. I moved twice in one year. I got divorced. I saw beloved projects fall through. I lost close friends and pets I loved. All of these low points in my life have been sudden and painful, but I've forced myself not to treat them like traumas. During each of these times, I chose to accept my new situation because I no longer work from a place of ego. I knew these disruptions were like my car wreck; a spiritual sign warning me that I had to become higher frequency. I chose to work with Spirit to help that happen. Uncoupling, death, upheaval, and failure isn't about me; it's about what Source wants for my life. Realizing *that* is the way to fight back and defend yourself when awful things come to pass.

In every transition in my life, big and small, I try to feel so aligned with a higher power and my calling that, when I make a decision, it's never from a place of defensiveness, hostility, or self-preservation. Essentially, I tell myself that the choices I make are never about *me* or how I might react; they're about doing what's best for the world and the people in it.

You might be saying to yourself, *Rachel, that all sounds good, but it's also pretty unrealistic. Breakups are tough. Getting fired or kicked out of your home is stressful. How can you* not *hate the person who did that to you or take it personally?* I know it's hard, but think of it in these terms: If one person in a relationship cheats on the other person, what hurts most is not the actual act, but the *reaction* to that act. It's the feeling you manifest that burns you inside, not the incident that caused it. Cheating is not something that's done *to* someone else; it's something that's simply done, and it's a symptom likely caused by feelings of worthlessness, rage, or some other destructive impulse. I want to be clear I'm not blaming the victim here. Betrayal is awful, and you don't have to accept or forgive it if that doesn't serve your own spirit. What I'm saying is that if you don't work from a place of ego, you realize that people aren't their symptoms; they're just people. What they do has nothing to do with the other individual. In essence, it's not about you or them. Like the bumper sticker says: *Shit happens.*

That's how I've come to feel about the lost friendships and broken relationships in my life. I'm not bitter; in fact, quite the opposite. I'm happy they happened, and that they ended, because I knew that we had reached the point where we'd completed whatever spiritual commitment we had made to each other. I can view the massive change that comes with the conclusion of a relationship as an opportunity; the other person gets the chance to do what brings them joy, and I can do the same. That's an incredibly positive situation, in my humble opinion, and it's coming right from Source.

I hope this doesn't make you think of me as someone incapable of human emotion. I know it's tough to be alive—and even tougher to avoid making decisions based on suffering and fear—because I take in my clients' pain when I exorcise them. I'm just now a little more bulletproof because I've experienced a lot, given what I do. I've had thousands of clients, most of whom are at their lowest and most vulnerable when they come to me, and I've relived their sexual abuse, suicide attempts, eating disorders, addictions, and more. Each and every single day I go to Source for the strength to help them. Having my senses tuned in to Spirit so closely, so often, has made it natural for me to rely on this communication in all parts of my life. Just as a mother still feels like Mom when she's not with her children, I'm someone who's in touch with Spirit even when I'm not actively talking to it.

I'm constantly upgrading my life, or, at least, that's how I choose to look at things. So much changes for me in the physical and the spiritual world all the time, so I know I need to be prepared for whatever might be coming next. I've got no other choice, really. To raise your frequency, fight off entities, and remain connected to Source, you have no other choice, either.

I've shed a million tears over lost or broken relationships, but I also enjoy being alone. Just the other morning I put the most awesome new sheets on my bed, cleaned my entire house, and replaced all my old, ratty bathroom towels with brand-new, fluffy ones. Then I started a fire in the fireplace, wrapped myself in a blanket, and watched horror movies on Netflix. It was just me, my dogs and cats, and no one to talk to me or ask anything of me. While I love my work, I'm Buffy 24/7, and feeling the weight of everyone's problems so deeply can be exhausting. Sometimes, you just need to channel that episode of *Buffy* when she leaves her hometown, becomes a diner waitress, and goes by her middle name, Anne. I always imagined her thinking, *No one knows me here; I'm just a hot chick in a polyester uniform.*

Sitting alone in my house, that's how I felt—minus the uniform. And, God, it was heaven.

I call where I now exist a high-minded place. It reminds me of standing tall on a mountain that you've spent days climbing, sweating, and straining the whole way. The view of the world below, so big and expansive, makes the ascent worthwhile. My perspective now is all-encompassing and beyond ego. I work from a 5-D consciousness that's been forged out of years of hard work and painful spiritual growth.

And, getting to the top of that mountain is something anyone can do. You don't have to become an exorcist, healer, or shaman. All of my clients leave my Spirit Room 1,000 times more high frequency than they were before, which gives them a launching point into high-mindedness. Becoming high-minded doesn't have to come from some radical life shift, or after enduring the pain of being plagued by entities. All you need to do is accept a new process of learning that allows you to adjust your attitudes and perspective.

Pretend you live in a house that you love. One day, while you're on vacation, lightning strikes your beautiful home and burns it down. You have two options in your response to such an event. You can feel devastated, lower than you've ever been in your life, berating the universe for conspiring against you. Or, you can choose to be high-minded in this situation, embracing the idea that the house was just not meant for you anymore. Spirit may even have been giving you clues about this, too. Maybe someone had recently fallen down your rickety front steps and gotten hurt. That was Source whispering in your ear, saying "This house isn't right for you anymore." Unfortunately, when you ignore that voice, Spirit will speak a little louder, perhaps giving you mold or making the plumbing go haywire. If you *still* don't pay attention, Spirit will finally give up and call forth a lightning bolt or something similarly devastating.

What you have to realize is that the disaster is not the problem; there was some underlying spiritual issue that made your home unsuitable. You just had to be told, somehow.

But what if you can't leave your house for financial reasons? Or because you live with your mother, who's so old she'd start declining if you moved her? Spirit doesn't care about these "logical" reasons. It doesn't want you to veer off your spiritual path, so it will be patient with you as long as you open yourself up. No matter what you believe your limitations are, you just have to listen to it, and you'll get the answer eventually. Spirit is in a constant state of expansion, and it wants to break the patterns that keep you confined in a negative state.

I'll give you a real-life example. Years ago, I had a client who'd had a truly terrible childhood. He'd been physically and sexually abused, and his mother was a drug addict, so she'd neglected him. He'd had to become the parent at home. He'd grown into a scarred adult who suffered from low self-esteem, so he was shy, lonely, and unable to speak to people. He was desperate to find love to make up for the insufficiencies he felt inside himself.

At the time, pickup artists were all the rage. "Mystery" was a household name, and Neil Strauss's *The Game,* which uncovered the culture of men who use unorthodox and manipulative methods to attract and seduce women, was an international bestseller. Now, I don't think all pickup artists are immoral, but my client had chosen to follow one who was. This guru's methods to get women into bed were disgusting, frankly, and he believed that putting women down was a great way to keep a girlfriend from leaving. My client fell for it hook, line, and sinker, started subtly insulting every woman he met at a bar or took on a date, and began to feel even worse. His now-lower self-esteem trapped him in a job he hated and kept him following this guru and looking for quick ego strokes in empty one-night stands, and he soon felt stuck in all aspects of his life.

He also suffered from volatile mood swings and a general feeling of a "dark cloud" over him, and he had a terrible time finishing projects he'd started. He also frequently experienced sleep paralysis and night terrors, which was affecting his ability to work.

Luckily, he had a friend who knew him (and me) well and suspected he might have an entity. He thought he'd benefit from seeing me, so he gave him my number. My client was initially hesitant, but then he called me up.

"I've been working with someone who's made me feel like I'm not myself," he said. "What he's teaching me is turning me into someone else. All I want in life is to find the right woman, and I want to do it with integrity."

"I can help you," I responded.

A few days later, he came in for an exorcism. When I saw him, it was clear there was something very wrong with him. He was gaunt and sunken. He hunched over the whole time I was speaking to him, and he looked exhausted, like he'd been sleeping badly for months. Misery was written all over his face, and he never laughed or smiled.

When I began his exorcism, Spirit sent me visual downloads about his childhood. Clear as day, I saw his mom lying on the couch, passed out because she was so high. I observed the man who'd touched him when he was just a boy. Then, as I burned blends and called in a few Higher Beings, I started to pull a Wraith from him—dark, shadowy, and connected to my client by a long, energetic cord. The bond between this entity and my client was especially strong, so I turned toward the area where I store my equipment and grabbed a long, ornate sword. Holding it in both of my hands, I waved it over my client's core, careful not to get too close to his skin. He gasped, and beads of sweat ballooned all over his face. I spotted the site of the etheric cord, and I cut it with the blade. Immediately my client exhaled heavily. He convulsed, first in his arms, then down his legs to his feet. I stood back, letting silence wash over the room as the Wraith dissipated. It had only been a half hour, yet the process was complete.

"How are you feeling?" I asked him after he sat up and pulled himself together.

"So different," he said. "Suddenly, I can see things clearly. None of my problems are about me. They don't control me; I'm the one who decides how to live my life."

The next day, he quit his job, and a month or so later, moved out of state. I talked to him recently, and he's found his dream job and is dating a woman who supports him, and whom he doesn't have to insult to keep interested. Imagine that!

Like so many others, his exorcism removed the blocks that prevented him from connecting with Source. In fact, his new, clear perspective was the very model of how to be high-minded.

Dealing with Others in a High-Minded Way

Don't expect that being high-minded and in touch with Spirit is going to make you the most popular person in the room, though. In fact, I know from personal experience that your newfound high frequency may be absolutely repellent to some.

Because I'm so hyperaware of what Spirit has to offer, I'm always buzzing with a very particular kind of high-frequency energy. Being high frequency manifests itself differently for each person, but it makes me exceedingly positive and optimistic— even when my circumstances are shitty. I'm direct and matter-of-fact, and I don't back down from things, which is a good quality for an exorcist to have, if you ask me! I'm also supersassy. Follow me on Instagram and you'll see.

People are like magnets, and they're drawn to each other based on the responses of their energy signatures. This explains why there are people in the world that you can't get enough of, while there are others whom you'd be happy to avoid for all time. If you appreciate someone's vibe, you tend to like them. If you're repelled by it, you probably won't be going on vacation with them.

Unfortunately, my energy tends to make some people a little insane. Sure, I have lots of friends and an overabundance of love and compassion for pretty much every human and animal I meet, but not everyone feels the same way about me. That's because these people are low frequency, and they don't travel on the wavelength I do. They haven't done the work to get there, and they subconsciously resent that I have. High frequency works like a mirror for those who are still low, creating jealousy, anger, and possessiveness, because they actually crave that light, but they're not ready to walk the path of it. They're not prepared to face their own pain, and they're upset at you for consistently showing them what they're missing.

That came up recently for me on a night out.

Every now and then, I go to this restaurant on Sunset Boulevard called the Rainbow Bar and Grill, which is right near Whiskey a Go Go. The Rainbow's been around since the early seventies, and it's the legendary hangout for rockers and groupies. Keith Moon, Alice Cooper, and John Lennon were all regulars during the seventies, and in the eighties it became the hair metal epicenter, filled with the members of Mötley Crüe, Guns N' Roses, Poison, and all the cocaine and hair spray you could imagine. It still attracts musicians and actors, and there's a club upstairs that books great acts.

It's not the eighties, and I'm not into blow, but I like going to the Rainbow. The food is good and the vibe is fun. Once, I was there with a group of people, and a fairly well-known actor, who was friends with one of my friends, sat down at our table. I'll call him Mr. Asshole. He was boisterous, loud, and high as a kite, and he kept making jokes that irritated the crap out of me. I could sense something dark about Mr. Asshole—something more off than just the drugs he was on—and I thought to myself, *Oh, man. This guy needs an exorcism really fucking badly.*

Of course, I didn't express my concern out loud. In fact, I tried to warm up to him, which wasn't easy since he was so annoying.

"Hey," I said to him as I reached my hand across the table and touched his arm. "I want to ask you something."

Now, this question had absolutely nothing to do with his dark energy or the fact that I could see entities swarming around him. I just wanted to ask him about a movie he had been in, something I'd actually liked, even though I didn't much like him. But Mr. Asshole looked at me with daggers in his eyes, stood up, and pushed his chair back so hard that it fell and slammed against the ground.

"Don't touch me," he said. "Don't you fucking touch me."

The whole table went silent, with me the quietest of them all. Then I muttered a half-hearted apology, even though, being high-minded, I knew I had nothing to be sorry about. My energy was clearly toxic to him, and Source had set off the spiritual equivalent of a smoke bomb between us.

I've had the same issue with people I work with, guys I go out on dates with, and family members of really close friends. I never actually *do* anything to them, but they're repelled by me from the moment they encounter me. Even people I've never met seem to hate me. I've gotten death threats online, been called "An Evil Devil Worshipper" via email, and been told more times than I can imagine—by total strangers, especially after the NPR piece that ran about me—that I'm a con artist. Social media can be a terrible cesspool, especially when people think you're in league with Satan. Sure, you could attribute this to simple trolling, or to some people's conservative belief systems, but I think it has more to do with my energy signature. Even though a person online may not have met me, they're so low frequency that they only see others through their perspective. It's easy to say, "Well, everyone sees others through their own lens," but I think those who are more self-aware and conscious are able to remove themselves from that equation and understand another person as they truly are.

I have a great group of female friends, but sometimes my relationships with women are tough as well. These friendships can run hot and cold, for reasons I cannot explain. I might have a friend with whom I become very close, very fast. In a matter of weeks, or months, she will decide she hates me. Sometimes she'll lash out at me, accuse me of doing something I didn't, or just disappear and never return my texts or calls.

It's never easy when this happens. I may have abilities beyond the average human being, but I'm still a person with emotions. But being high-minded means accepting things and moving on, so I tell myself: *I'm going to give myself one day of grief, and keep going. I can't help who I am.* Then I'll take a walk, remember that there's more to life than spiritually doomed friendships and pretty—but weird—guys, and pull myself together. Life and Spirit move on.

The Most High-Minded Creatures of All

As I've said, we are all born 100 percent in touch with Source. It's our creator, our nurturer, and the gift that keeps giving—but only if you decide to look to it for answers.

Babies and young children know this intrinsically because they're so much closer than adults to the point at which they came into the world, unsullied. If they're lucky, they haven't faced the sort of traumas that disrupt a person's connection to Spirit, so they see the universe through spiritually colored glasses. They expect the best of people, talking freely to strangers on the street and making friends with any new child they meet on the playground or in preschool.

Their connections aren't all emotional, either. Many kids younger than three see spirits, have imaginary friends, or talk about their past lives quite openly. They might describe in detail what their new friends or old memories look like, how they make them feel, or what their names are. I saw spirits when I was a child, so I believe intrinsically that none of those things and beings are figments of a young imagination. If you think about it, why would a child make these up? To impress you? How would they know to do so? Kids this young aren't even aware of the difference between make-believe and reality. Instead, they're deeply connected to Source, because no person or traumatic experience has told them not to be.

Unfortunately, too many adults strip Spirit away from children. A young girl might say to her mother, "I see someone living in the mirror on my wall," and be told to stop making up stories. When the adult does this, she crushes Spirit, teaching her daughter to be a skeptical—even pessimistic—person who's driven only by her intellect. She disconnects her from what's most pure in the world. Then as the little girl grows up, she may begin to feel negative emotions, and in her teens she might experiment with sex, drugs, or anything that gives her the sensation of reconnecting to Spirit. When those things don't undo her negative feelings, she might become hostile, angry, or fearful.

Of course, that's when entities descend and try to attach.

This is why I drop everything if I get a call about a child who needs an exorcism. Kids are innocent, and they deserve to exist on the high-minded place from which they originated.

Animals aren't so different, and I understand their connection to Source because I've witnessed it with my own two eyes.

I live with many animals. My oldest dog is fifteen, and my oldest cat is about the same, and I love them and their five housemates more than almost anything in the world. I'm an absolute sucker for pets, so if someone I know announces that a friend of a friend found an abandoned dog on the side of the road, I'll probably take it in that night.

I adore animals not just because they're cute and furry and, most of the time, easier to deal with than people, but also because they're so high frequency. Like children, they expect the best of everyone, and even when they're in pain or suffering, they're gracious. Their owner might leave them outside in the cold overnight, or hit them for no reason, yet they'll still look up at them with big, innocent eyes and plead for that person to be kind to them. After getting burned one too many times they might cower when a human approaches them, but as soon as they get some good scratches behind the ears, all is forgiven and forgotten.

Because they're so close to Source, animals also don't attract entities. Animals definitely see them, though, and if I'm in a room with one of my pets when an entity passes through, I can watch his gaze follow the entity's path. But never, not once, has an entity stopped, turned around, and tried to attach to one of my brood.

Many years ago I had a cat named Isis. I'd adopted her when I lived in Florida and found her in a parking lot crouched under my car. She was so scared that I couldn't bear to shoo her off, so I went to a local pet store, bought a carrier, and with the help of one of the store's employees, lured her into it. I drove her to the vet, who announced that she was pregnant. I took her home, midwifed a litter of kittens, and soon adopted them out. Isis followed me to Colorado, then LA, and was with me as I began my journey to performing exorcisms.

A few years ago, a friend of mine had a Wraith. Like all entities, Wraiths are attached to you, but unlike many others, they're not actually *in* your body. Instead, they have a long cord that extends from their form into yours, allowing them to move around space without interruption. The cord resembles a tentacle, or in some cases, multiple tentacles. The entity never travels far and certainly never disconnects because it needs to keep feeding.

One night, when my friend was visiting, Isis came out from a hiding spot under a table, saw the Wraith floating through the space near my friend, and absolutely lost her mind. Her fur shot up, and she began growling and hissing, like she was gearing up for a catfight.

"What the hell is wrong with your cat?" my friend asked, confused. He'd never seen Isis behave this way.

Of course, I knew the answer, but I refused to say, "Well, it's because you have this nasty entity extending out from you, and if you don't let me exorcise it, she's going to continue freaking out." I *never* try to push my friends into exorcisms. Ultimately, coming to see me to deal with your demons is your decision, and while I may gently imply that you may need my services, I'll never guilt or scare you into using them.

"She just senses something she doesn't like that's near you," I finally said. "We can talk about it if you like."

Poor Isis started losing her hair that night. It fell off in clumps as she began to lick herself obsessively. She was a stressed-out mess, the likes of which I'd never seen before. My friend continued to come over, just as he always had, and Isis was almost hairless within a few weeks.

Finally, I decided to push my friend toward a decision.

"Look," I said, "you have a low-level entity, and if you'd like I can remove it. This would help Isis as much as you."

Thankfully, he agreed with me, and after his exorcism, he and Isis felt better right away. My poor old cat's hair grew back in a few weeks, in fact.

I can't prove this, but I strongly believe that there's a link between trauma and an animal's ability to see entities. Isis had been abandoned while she was pregnant, and her awareness—and fear of—my friend's Wraith was acute. I have a dog named Izzy who is so sensitive to energy that she's anxious all the time, holing herself away in her crate at the end of the day, then staying there all night. I've watched her when there are entities in the room with her, and she seizes up, then darts into her crate. I know she sees *everything*, and I think it's no coincidence that she had a terrible life when she was young. For her first four years, she was an abused backyard breeder dog, living in horrendous conditions, giving birth to babies again and again and watching them ripped away from her weeks too soon. She experienced trauma, and now she's all too aware of beings that feed off what comes out of tragedy.

I can't say for sure whether this holds true for humans, too, but I don't believe so, mainly because I've had many clients who've experienced terrible traumas yet can't see entities. Animals are purer, and they live in the present, through their Heart Space, more easily than we do, which is why I think they can see things we can't.

Animals have a much wider range of knowledge than anyone

gives them credit for. Much as they can sense when a person is sad, or have been known to detect tumors or illnesses before they've been diagnosed, they can perceive subtle energy shifts in the way many humans can't because they're coming from a place of ego. Animals will go up to a person and growl at them, and no one will know why. It's because they don't like that person's energy.

This doesn't just happen with dogs or cats, either. Pigs, cows, and horses are highly intelligent creatures, and they go back into Source after they die just like humans do. They're innocent and spiritually pure, and for that reason, I've tried for years to stay away from animal products. There's just so much suffering in the meat, egg, and dairy industry, and at this point in my life, I've moved to such a high-minded place that I really don't want to be a part of that.

Now that you have a clear sense of what an entity is, what motivates it, and, most important, how Source plays into that ecosystem, let's move on to how I perform exorcisms.

CHAPTER 7

The Ins and Outs of Exorcisms

N ow that I've been performing exorcisms for almost ten years, I've learned a few things. First, that entities aren't as strong as you might imagine. They might look like the stuff of nightmares, and make you feel like you've been drained of the essence of life—but in reality, they aren't as horrible as they want you to believe. That's one of the reasons I can *always* remove them.

Second, everyone's exorcism is completely different. I've done some exorcisms that lasted less than half an hour and took only a little of my energy, and some that spanned two days and left me utterly spent for more than a month. Most last about an hour, however, and all end with the glorious destruction of an entity.

Finally, I've learned that even though no two exorcisms are alike, almost all follow the same basic pattern. Because of this, I've developed my own blueprint for fighting them.

Who I See

I don't have a fancy website, a toll-free number, a dedicated, exorcist-specific Facebook page, or even an office. Instead, all my clients find me through word of mouth, so I typically know something about them when they come to meet me. Even though I may not have met them, there's a good chance I'll have a notion of what they do, where they like to spend their downtime, or even what they've been going through in their personal lives. In some cases, I'll have next to no information. To be honest, this is my preference, for the reasons I'll describe below.

Well over half of my clients are high-profile celebrity types, so almost everything about them can be found online, in the tabloids, or even on the national news. These are busy people, so I may know a month in advance that I'm going to be meeting them. But in that time, I try very, very hard not to expose myself to anything about them. I don't watch their movies, and I don't google them. I even steer clear of conversations where their names might come up. I don't just avoid public information, though; I also try not to let even the slightest thought of these very public figures enter my head.

Why do I go to these lengths? Because I want their exorcisms to be authentic. Everything I learn about the person during their exorcism should come from Spirit. During an exorcism, I feel out facts about a client's life—whether they're having relationship problems or that they were sexually abused as a child—

and that information can't be clouded by outside influences or information.

Coincidentally, I put on blinders when I write as well. When I'm working on a book or a screenplay, I won't read anything that has even the slightest connection with what I'm putting on the page. I want my words to come purely from Spirit, unaffected by anyone else's work.

Honestly, I don't care who you are when you set up an appointment with me. You could be the mousiest, most insignificant person in the world, who hasn't left her house or contributed to society in the last ten years, but if you need my help, I can't wait to make things better for you. I also don't ask for payment. I charge by donation only, because I believe everyone—rich, middle class, or desperately poor—deserves to live their best life, entity-free.

All I need from a client is for them to be 100 percent willing. If your husband has forced you to make an appointment with me against your deepest wishes, my methods will not be effective. I often receive calls from folks saying something like, "My brother is such a problem. He's so dark and toxic, and he's ripping my family apart because of his actions. Yet, he doesn't want to change. Can you help him?" I'm so sorry, but I cannot. That kind of work is not a good use of my time. Your brother has to *want* to see me. Otherwise he's going to resist his exorcism emotionally, spiritually, and psychologically, and even though I might kill myself removing his entities, he's going to walk out the door and immediately welcome those forces right back because he hasn't changed his own energy.

Let me be crystal clear, however, that being willing is very different than being open. I meet many people who are closed up for whatever reason. They may have been abandoned as children, they may have deep-seated trust issues, have been abused or be painfully shy by nature. They might simply be skeptical about me, believing that no one (especially a tattooed "exorcist" wearing a skull T-shirt) can truly help them. As long as they are willing to open up to the idea that I might help, then I'm eager to try.

When I meet with closed-off clients, I know their exorcism is going to be exhausting and tough. Either they're so full of malevolent entities that I won't be able to see the source of the darkness inside them, or they're so guarded that they're going to repeatedly resist opening up to me. In the first case, I know I'll always succeed and perform a top-notch exorcism—it's just going to take me a little longer. But in the second case, I'll need my client to work with me. I may ask them if they're nervous about what's about to happen, and then explain the process. Or I'll talk about myself and use examples from my life to put them at ease.

Sometimes I'll share information I'm getting from Spirit that's specific about them. Nine times out of ten my clients are surprised and emotional when they hear this, so I try to speak in general terms. I don't want them to feel on the spot, bombarded, or on guard. I'll say, "Often, people experience this when this happens" instead of being specific and mentioning their exact situation. They need to feel comfortable, so I may also light a fire or candles in my Spirit Room to create atmosphere. Then I might explain everything they're about to experience. I coax them to let their guard down and trust, even the tiniest bit. If I can sense, deep down, that a client is happy to unleash the entities that have been plaguing them, they're going to walk out of my Spirit Room a changed person.

Why and How I Do What I Do: The Nitty-Gritty

I honestly don't much care about my reputation, and it's not because, as a nondenominational exorcist, I'm pretty much the only game in town. If people think I'm a fraud, I'm not bothered in the least. I know I'm not. And when my clients come out of an exorcism feeling better than they have in years, *they* know I'm not. In my book, that's all the proof anyone needs.

I need to be as egoless as possible in everything I do because, if I am, I'm more likely to be guided by Spirit. Source holds the essential truths of how to better a person's life. It wants my client—and during your exorcism, me—to embrace what will help him or her improve, heal, and thrive. If I can't be an egoless vessel who connects to Spirit without interruption, I'm not doing my job successfully, and I'm not going to be able to clear out entities.

Authenticity isn't just about being spiritually fit, though. I also need to feel physically well—but doesn't mean treating my body like a temple. Juice cleanses aren't for everyone, and you don't need to be "pure" to connect to Spirit. So while I eat well and exercise, I'm human. I eat pizza. I drink scotch. I just try to keep myself generally healthy so I'm clearheaded. That also goes for sleep. When I set up a meeting with a client, I insist that it occur at a time when I'm well rested. I won't do an exorcism late at night—or, God forbid, in the middle of the night—unless it's an emergency.

Spirit sends me messages about future clients before they come in for their exorcism—sometimes months in advance, other times the week or day of their exorcism, and other times right when they step into my house. It's always different. Spirit might pass on random, hard-to-pinpoint information like colors or feelings, or I might receive a message from one of their deceased relatives that relates to the kind of person they are or what they're going through. For example, if I have a client who was adopted (which I may or may not know already), their biological grandmother or mother—or anyone who's passed and is connected to their initial abandonment—might visit me a week or two in advance to give me hints about what my client may be struggling with or the old traumas that are pulling him or her down. If a deceased spirit is particularly powerful, they may even come to me months beforehand.

Sometimes, setting up an appointment with a client is a real struggle, especially with busy celebrities. Their assistants will be adamant that their boss can only see me at one very particular time, and that kind of conversation never goes well.

"Let's do next Thursday. She's got a shoot at seven A.M., then a lunch at noon, and a meeting with her agent at five, so it has to be three and can't go more than an hour and a half," the assistant will tell me.

"It has to be at four," I'll respond.

"Four P.M. is never going to work."

"Then pick another day, because I know for sure that four is the only time for this."

Click. Then they'll call back ten minutes later, with their boss's schedule clear as day.

I'm a bossy lady, but I don't act this way because I want to be in charge. I make these demands because Spirit has told me that 4 P.M. is *the* time when this particular client will be most open and receptive to being cleansed. It's the precise hour that Source will give me the tools and guidance to rid them of their entities.

I don't care who you are or how many demands there are on your time. If you need my help, you have to listen to what I'm saying. I haven't always had this gift—Spirit gave it to me over time—but now it's particularly acute.

Depending on the client and the issues they're facing—as revealed by the messages I've received from Spirit—I'll give instructions about what to do before an exorcism. I tell some people to meditate beforehand, and I tell others not to eat meat. I insist that a lot of my clients fast the day before, and I tell others not to wear metal because it emanates a particular frequency.

When a client comes to my house, I take them out back to my Spirit House, which is where I work even when I'm not performing exorcisms. Los Angeles is an expensive place to live, and, for me, even more so because exorcisms have to occur in a space with a separate entrance. My work is dangerous, and I don't want to subject my pets—or my home—to other people's low frequencies or the dark energies of entities during an exorcism. It's best to have a space outside that's its own room (like a pool house or guest cottage) so that the energy can be contained until it's destroyed.

I didn't figure this out right away; it took time and experience. I had a few clumsy exorcisms where items moved around the room, there were dozens of strange noises, and my mood went up and down just a bit too much. These were mostly annoying incidents caused by minor entities, but I soon realized that if I controlled the environment of my Spirit Room, I could stabilize an exorcism to a certain degree. In the beginning of my career I didn't set up my Spirit Room to contain energy, so it traveled out the door and into my house, which wasn't ideal. I also put all my candles on plates, and I knocked into them all the time, got wax everywhere, and set things (including myself) on fire. Now I always enclose candles in lanterns.

I prefer a place with an apex roof, simply because it makes the room feel bigger, but it's not necessary. I just move around a lot—especially on the perimeter of a client's body—so it's best that I don't feel cramped. I also need somewhere where I can fit a queen-size bed and built-in shelving for all my "equipment." I use herb blends, incense, candles, crystals, and stones during exorcisms, and I need somewhere to store them that's within my reach. I even have a sword and dagger stashed away near my tools. As I did with my client who'd fallen for a pickup artist's scams, I may use them to symbolically cut energetic connections between a very malevolent entity and its host.

Scattered around my Spirit Room are lanterns, godlike idols and statues, skulls, ceremonial masks from many cultures, and paintings with religious iconography. These items all have particular meaning to me, and Spirit channels itself through all of them. I've found all of them at yard sales, or I've happened upon them while I was out doing something else, and just the other day I was at the Rose Bowl Flea Market and found a *magnificent* table with angels and roses painted on it. It's from the 1940s. When I asked Spirit, "Why do I need this?" it told me, "Because it was used by a tarot reader in a traveling carnival. She read cards on it." It has a drawer, and that's where I now keep my own tarot deck.

I have to have a bathroom a few steps away because, unfortunately, exorcisms can be messy work. I estimate that one out of every ten clients vomits after or during theirs, and they certainly don't want to do that in a paper bag or bucket. They're often embarrassed by this, even though I try to put them at ease. When I tell clients I've seen it all, that's exactly what I mean. And I can tell you a bathroom is necessary.

◎

Regina Carpinelli is the founder and president of Stan Lee's Los Angeles Comic Con, which is one of the largest comic cons in America and one of the biggest annual pop culture gatherings in Los Angeles. I've been a guest at this amazing event since 2011, and Regina and I have become dear friends. Early on in our working relationship, I revealed to her what I do, and it got her thinking. I'll let her tell you the rest in her own words.

REGINA

When Rachel told me what she did on the side, I thought, Okay, that's fun. In this business, you meet all types, so I just didn't think much of it.

At the time, though, I was going through some really difficult problems. I had way too many people around me who were abusive, and I was self-medicating. I'd become depressed, sometimes even suicidal, and my life felt like a big, huge burden. Finally, I spoke to Rachel about it. She responded, "I can help. Let's do an exorcism."

I believe in spirituality, but, honestly, I can't tell you who out there is crazy and who's not. It's not something I ever really put my mind to. But at that point, I was up for anything, so I said yes.

Rachel told me to fast the day before my exorcism, so I did as I was told. When I went over to her house, she asked me to lie down on a bed and close my eyes. Over the course of the next hour, she did her thing. She burned incense, said words I couldn't really understand, and waved her hands around. As she was doing all of this, I began feeling the weirdest sensations; it was like something was being pulled out of me. I just lay there and let whatever was happening happen, and then, finally, Rachel commanded that an entity come out.

Immediately, I jumped out of the bed I'd been lying on and ran to the bathroom, sick as a dog.

Bear in mind, I hadn't eaten anything for a full twenty-four hours. There was absolutely nothing in my stomach. But when I looked down into the toilet, I saw the strangest thing: lying there at the bottom of the bowl were two black jellyfish.

Now, I'm a practical person. I also believe in science. If I were going to vomit after a day of not eating, what would come out of me would be bile. There was no bile down there; all I saw were two dark, translucent blobs with little tentacles coming out of them.

I couldn't explain it then, and I still can't, but all I can say is that I felt immediately better.

I went back to Rachel's Spirit Room a year later for a tune-up and to face some childhood trauma I'd been holding in, and I followed the same routine as the year before. I fasted for a full day. I lay on a bed. Rachel did her thing. And, sure enough, at the end of all of it, I had to jump up and vomit.

This time, I saw what looked like little pieces of wood in the bottom of the toilet bowl. You know when you put down ground cover, but it's not mulch, it's wood chips or small sticks? That's what was down there.

But just like a year before, I immediately felt better, and I kept feeling that way. I was emotionally lighter and happier. I always used to hold tension in my back, and now I don't. I didn't clear the toxic people out of my life right away, but within a year, I did. Seeing Rachel was more helpful than therapy and gave me a different kind of empowerment. When unhealthy friends or family try to wedge themselves into my life now, I know how to block them out, and I do it. Now I have great relationships.

I like having windows in my Spirit Room because it helps to have some sort of ventilation. Fresh air in, bad feelings out. I also need to have air-conditioning because it gets *very* hot during an exorcism. Even at night, the room will heat up an extra ten degrees at a minimum. Now, I don't have a scientific explanation for this, but it must be because of the amount of energy flowing around the room. It's a fucking cauldron within minutes. Like I said, I have a fireplace to create a mood, but during many exorcisms, it gets so hot I can't ignite it.

You have to have great light during an exorcism as well. This is not because I need it to be bright to work. It comes down to energy. You know the energy of a room when you see it, and good lighting always helps. If it's a bright, cheerful space, I'm immediately drawn to it, and entities are immediately repelled. The only time this doesn't matter is when I have an exorcism at night; then the light needs to be extremely low, and I typically work through candlelight or the glow of a fire, which bring in cleansing energy and higher being energy.

As I've said before, I don't allow anyone else but the client into my Spirit Room. This is even the case with children, so unfortunately, sometimes I have to cajole them—and reassure their parents—that they'll be safe all alone with me. It's simply too dangerous to have another individual in the room during an exorcism for two reasons. The first is that a person will be spiritually opened up if they're too close to what I'm doing. Their body and soul will be in a sort of limbo, and if they don't go through a full exorcism, they'll walk out of the room energetically vulnerable and become a magnet for entities.

Think of it this way: Imagine you fall asleep, and at the very deepest part of your sleep cycle, someone or something jolts you awake. Chances are you're going to feel terrible for at least a few minutes. Those five, ten, or twenty minutes are not the time to drive a car, operate heavy machinery, or make any rational decisions. You need to go through the process of clearing out the mind fog that leaves you feeling half-asleep, half-awake.

The second reason is that if there's another person in the room during an exorcism, my client may not feel comfortable answering my questions about why they've come to me. Everyone who sees me has secrets—and most reveal them—and I spend a lot of time uncovering and then talking about what's plaguing them before I do my work. You wouldn't bring your husband to therapy with you, would you? Especially if your husband is one of the reasons you decided to see a therapist in the first place? Not in a million years.

When someone is comfortable and situated in the room, I acknowledge what a big step they've made.

"Being here today is huge," I say. "*So* many things in your life had to align for you to come to me." Then I usually look right in their eyes, deadly serious. "For next hour or so, you're at a crossroads. I'm going to take out everything that's been in you up to this point."

Then I ask my clients why they've come to me. They usually start to unpack all the problems they've been having lately, and I follow their every word. But here's the funny part: *I never actually listen to them.* I may nod my head and smile while they speak, but in reality I've totally tuned them out.

Please don't hate me for this. It's not that I don't care about my clients; it's just that they're not the best judges of what's *actually* happening within their lives. I get a lot of "my ex-wife is doing this or that," but the anger a client feels is just a symptom of a greater spiritual problem. Feelings aren't facts, and emotions can be a part of ego, so the messy angst surrounding someone's domestic situation (or lack thereof) isn't reality.

My clients don't know this truth, so that's why I look to their Spirit Guides, Master Teachers, ancestors, or the deceased relatives who've visited me before their exorcism for answers.

CHAPTER 8

Higher Beings

Spirit Guides, Master Teachers, Ancestors, and More

M any people have asked what drives me during an exorcism. Am I powerless, entirely under the sway of Source? Am I some otherworldly creature, like an angel? Or do I work completely through intuition?

"Intuition" and Source are the same in my understanding. People often don't believe this, but I know this to be the case because Spirit's communicated it to me directly. It's led me to that understanding. When you hear a voice in your head telling you to make one choice over another, you may think this stems from your own thoughts or "intuition." Maybe you don't trust this voice because you don't trust yourself, but you should. Know that Spirit speaks to people in this way. We're all divine on some level, constantly working with Spirit.

When you open yourself up to Spirit's guidance, you'll be amazed at all that it can provide. In my case, Source has given me access to a wealth of Higher Beings, including Spirit Guides, Master Teachers, ancestors, gods and goddesses, and more—all of whom are invaluable in my work as an exorcist.

You may be thinking: *Now wait a second, Rachel. I know you see entities. And you mentioned a while ago you saw dead people, too. But there are others?* Yes, many others in fact. When I perform an exorcism, I don't do so alone. I call in any number of Higher Beings, who come to me directly from Source. They don't just provide *me* guidance, either; they're with each and every one of you, available to assist you at any point you might need.

I know this sounds outlandish, but it's totally logical. If you're walking around with entities attached to you, sucking away your strength, it would follow that you'd also have something positive going with you through life too, right? Absolutely. I call these beautiful beings "High Vibrational Entities," and they include religious figures like Jesus, Muhammad, and the Archangel Michael, gods and goddesses who you might have thought were just the stuff of mythology (they're not), Spirit Guides who may or may not have a name, and even your long-dead ancestors.

I'm not the only person who makes her living in the spiritual space to use the term Higher Beings; throughout recent history shamans, New Age gurus, theologians, and more have referred to Master Teachers, Spirit Guides, and others I use in my taxonomy. And, of course, the notion of High Vibrational Entities has existed since ancient times. But I believe that the way I describe, experience, and use them is mine and mine alone.

Before I describe each of these Higher Beings in detail, let me finish explaining how they—through Spirit—give me a window into a client's heart, mind, and soul even before I ask them to lie down in my Spirit Room. As I've mentioned, I'm often visited by a High Vibrational Entity or two in the weeks or months before I first meet a client. When that person does come to me, I either see those same Higher Beings or other Spirit Guides, who appear and then speak right over my client, whispering in my mind the real trauma that's caused the attachment that's necessitated an exorcism. *Her parents died when she was a child,* they'll say, channeling Spirit. Or they'll go into deep detail, explaining how being raised by a busy aunt and uncle, who already had multiple children of their own, left my client feeling neglected. Spirit Guides have a desire to reveal the root of a problem; after all, sometimes you have to tear down and rebuild the foundations of a structure in order to make it stronger.

Oftentimes the messages I receive are so powerful that I'll interrupt a client while they're talking about their difficulty with love, their inability to keep a job, or whatever else is eating at them. I used to be hesitant about doing this because I didn't want to upset a client while they were so vulnerable, but after years and years of knowing that Spirit Guides are far more clued in than my clients, I've gotten pretty ballsy.

"Stop," I'll say. "You're not here because you hate your boss. Let's cut to the chase. Your issues started decades ago. Here's what's really happening."

Nine times out of ten, people appreciate my candor, even if it's not what they expected or if they're shocked. In fact, I find that being 100 percent bullshit-free really breaks down barriers. My clients know immediately that I mean business. More than that, they understand right away that I'm in touch with them on a deeper level than they ever believed possible.

My clients exist on many layers of consciousness. There are some who are almost completely self-aware and won't argue with me when I tell them what their Spirit Guides have revealed to me. Others look at me confused or even in shock. They're what I call the "slow pots to boil." They're less in touch with their feelings for sure, and more unconscious, and they may take a while to warm up to what I've revealed to them. Their exorcism will likely take a little longer and be harder, too. Yet, afterward, when they're feeling happier and lighter, they almost always agree that I was right in what I said. I've had incredibly famous celebrities sit down in my Spirit Room and deny backward and forward that they're having relationship troubles. But after their exorcism, they'll admit, "You know, I'm actually about to file for divorce."

I already knew this, of course, because their Spirit Guides told me.

I once performed an exorcism on a very famous musician. I can't name him, but I can tell you that he has millions and millions of fans, is an entrepreneur, and demonstrates a tremendous amount of compassion for the planet. I'll call him Mr. Big Heart. Mr. Big Heart had heard about me through a friend, and he'd decided he might have an entity because he'd become so disinterested in music. What had once been his passion had become a burden. He assumed his creative impulses were being stifled by something larger, so he called me up.

When he came for his exorcism, we didn't talk much about music. Using information I'd received from Spirit, I began to ask

Mr. Big Heart about his relationships, and he was candid. He said he worried—just as lots of uberfamous individuals do—that people wanted to be close to him because he had so much money and power.

"I don't want to be taken advantage of," he said. "People assume I'm bulletproof because of who I am and what I'm capable of doing—not to mention what I've done—but I'm not. I've been lied to, stolen from, cheated on, accused of horrible things, and sued for almost everything. I just wish I could know that my friendships are genuine."

"I imagine that's hard," I responded.

"It's awful. I want people in my life, but it's tough to be close to anyone. I've been famous for so long, but I feel like no one knows me because I'm terrified to open myself up. Making a real connection has been so frightening for me, for years."

I heard what Mr. Big Heart was saying, but I wasn't listening to all the details. I was paying more attention to his Spirit Guides, who had started speaking to me.

There's a woman who really, truly loves him, they said. *They've been close for a long time, and she's genuine.* Then they revealed specific details about her that would allow my client to recognize her.

I found the source of his trauma, which was rooted in childhood suffering, and exorcised the Wraith that had attached to him. Then I told him about his lady friend, and he smiled.

"That's good to know," he said. "I've been so lonely."

I don't know whether he'll pursue a relationship with her, but at least he has some comfort in understanding he has a true friend in the world.

SPIRIT GUIDES

Let's get a little more specific about Spirit Guides. They are the lowest-level Higher Beings. It's not that they aren't spiritually powerful; they just don't watch over the world at large in the way that other Higher Beings do. Their work is specific to individuals. They're always with you, just following you or floating nearby. They've been assigned to you by Spirit, and they're at your disposal for whenever you need them. I always joke that they must have the worst jobs in the world, latched on to people who don't recognize they're there and never listen to the messages they're sending. But, trust me, they're there, and they know everything about your past and your present. They essentially represent Spirit, so any guidance they'll offer is pure Source energy. They're working in your best interests at all times.

Spirit Guides look more like regular people than some of the other Higher Beings such as Master Teachers, gods, and goddesses. They have a glow to them, like angels, and very soft, gentle facial features. I like to think of them as "light beings"— unadulterated, good energy whose power is always more spiritual than physical.

I'm deeply in tune with my own Spirit Guides, but I don't differentiate them. In fact, I see them as one unit. I never ask their names or even identify them individually, but I suppose if I did, they might give themselves a name they think I'd like. After all, they're there to help me.

During an exorcism, though, I tend to leave my Spirit Guides alone, turning only to those of my clients. That's because I need a window into their lives, not my own. I mostly use my Spirit Guides when I'm performing what I call a ritual, which is any kind of spiritual practice I do while I am alone: burning incense, handling my crystals, or bringing in the energies of fire, water, earth, and air by lighting candles or ringing chimes. I do this on days when I think I need a spiritual boost, which isn't every day because I like to be respectful of my Guides. We have a working relationship, so I'm mindful not to bombard them with questions all day long because no one—not even spiritual beings—has endless patience. When I bring them in, I also thank them and offer gifts like food, wine, and coins. At this point in my life, I don't need my Spirit Guides for hard-hitting answers or bare-knuckle guidance; I've honed my connection to Source so much that I can go straight to there, not requiring a go-between.

MASTER TEACHERS

Master Teachers are higher up the food chain than Spirit Guides. They inhabit their own space, and you can access them if you need them, but they don't necessarily follow you. They're a bit more powerful than Spirit Guides, so their guidance tends to be more profound. I have no idea how or why they exist in a higher place than Spirit Guides, but since my frequency is so much lower than theirs, perhaps it's not my place to ask. Some shit I'm just never going to know.

I've been familiar with two of my Master Teachers since I was a teenager, but I didn't really acknowledge them until my early thirties. Even when I was hiding from them, I always felt comfortable with them, and part of me understood that they served a purpose. Deep down, I knew they were with me for good. They still appear to me anytime I need them, and they do so quickly. In fact, they're the Higher Beings I feel more of a kinship with than any other.

My first Master Teacher is masculine, and he's quite large—nearly the height of two people. He has the head of a man and the body of a goat from the neck down. He has two legs, so he's satyr-like, but he always remains upright.

This Master Teacher always tells me his name—Jameson—when he appears to me, and I've always thought this was funny. I mean, *of course* I remember who he is. It would be impossible to forget him, given that he's the only half man, half goat in my life! Also, most beings—human and otherwise—don't introduce themselves to you *every single time* you see them. I'm positive Jameson isn't his actual name, though, which might explain his formality. In the Spirit world, he's likely called something that a person like me can't pronounce or understand.

The other Master Teacher I call upon frequently is named Amelia, and she looks like a human woman who's dressed in all white. The only thing that sets her apart is that Amelia has no face. She's clearly a woman, but I can't make out her eyes, nose, cheeks, or mouth. She's just . . . blank.

Amelia and Jameson don't just help me with the big questions in my life. Sometimes, they're there to give me a spiritual pep talk or bolster me up when I'm not feeling my best. They'll do so without prompting, too. For example, I have days when I have one too many clients, and by 7 p.m., when I still have one more person to see, I'll think, *I can't. I just can't.*

That's when Amelia or Jameson will pop in and say, "We will do this for you." As we call in high-frequency energy together during the exorcism, they'll do the bulk of the heavy lifting, pulling out the entities for me.

My Master Teachers are also very generous, and often bestow me with gifts. I don't mean a nice new car or a boyfriend who sends me flowers every week. I'm talking about the subtle yet unmistakable signs that allow me to know that whatever decision I'm about to make is the right one. They also offer spiritual gifts. For example, when they recognize that I need strength, they may symbolically offer me a sword, causing an image of one to enter my mind.

Amelia and Jameson are the Higher Beings who sent the feathers to me for those seven days. They also tend to give me "feeling" gifts like energy, love, and courage. Their assistance is more personal than that which comes from Spirit. They're sort of like my spiritual parents—the first responders to the blazing inferno that's sometimes my life. They're there to clear the path so I can walk without fear.

ANCESTORS

Ancestors are exactly who you think they'd be. They're the men and women from whom you've descended, the family you've never met who have been dead for hundreds of years. They could be the British woman who came over on the *Mayflower*, signaling your family's official arrival in America, or someone far older, like an ancient man who lived in Babylonia. For whatever reason, these ancestors decide to follow you through life, and though it's unlikely you'll ever be aware of them, they do guide you based on whatever their interest or your need is. I know I have ancestors following me—everyone does—but I've chosen to leave them in peace and have never asked them to identify themselves. I just understand who they are because I see and feel them and have my entire life.

It's hard to describe, but I can distinguish ancestors from other Higher Beings not just through their appearance, but because of a feeling I've learned directly from Spirit. Think of it this way: If a deeply religious person goes to a house of worship, they feel elated. Their heart swells with happiness. With each level of Higher Being, I get a certain amount of that feeling. The more benevolent the Higher Being, the bigger the sensation. It also works the other way; the more malevolent an entity is, the worse I'll feel.

During exorcisms, I often become aware of who my clients' ancestors are. For example—and brace yourself because this is a little odd—I ran into a Celtic warrior woman during a recent exorcism. After I called her into the room, she revealed that, in her life, she'd secretly helped women who'd been raped. She stayed with my client, protecting her, because that woman had been in a few precarious, frightening situations with the men in her life, and she needed a solid force of female strength around her. Even before my client opened her mouth to tell me why she'd come to see me, the Celtic warrior woman from yesteryear gave me a window into the true nature of the woman's hurt. With a sharper eye to the sight of the trauma, the exorcism was much easier.

I once had a male client—a Wall Street investor—whose Viking ancestor revealed himself during his descendant's exorcism. These two men, separated by thousands of years, existed in vastly different realms, but in many ways they were just different versions of the same hypermasculine figure. One was a leader in battle, the other was a warrior on the trading floor. The Viking spirit helped my client in business and was instrumental in revealing the source of my client's issues, which centered around anxiety and an inability to trust himself and his abilities.

Ancestors are like Spirit Guides because they like to help steer you in the right direction. They'll visit you whenever you appeal to them. But the difference is that ancestors were once alive, as human beings, on this planet. Most Guides haven't been. Ancestors carry a familial DNA-based connection with you, as well as a soul family connection, meaning that they're often spirits you'll be incarnated with in different lifetimes. This is because, after *you* die, you may come back with a bit (or all) of these ancestors in you. How exactly, you ask? In addition to DNA that carries biological instructions for your body's development, each and every one of us carries spiritual DNA that directs our soul's growth.

RELIGIOUS BEINGS

As I said earlier in this book, I don't work through any specific set of religious beliefs. I wasn't raised in any faith, so I came into this calling with no preconceived notions about how entities related to religion. But that doesn't mean I'm not able to connect with a client for whom religion is important. I respect all beliefs, and more than that, I honor the good people who follow them. If a deeply Christian person walks into my Spirit Room—someone who loves Jesus more than life itself—who am I to argue that Christ isn't with them? He's influencing every part of this person's being. My client is full of Jesus. And that's just fine with me if they're living their life well.

Beyond that, I certainly know Jesus exists because I've seen

Him and felt His presence, which is just as Divine as you'd expect it to be. So, even though I'm not religious, I'm very connected to these incredible Higher Beings.

I'm a nondenominational exorcist, so I never deliberately invoke Jesus or any other figure associated with the world's major religions. But that doesn't mean they don't visit me—both during exorcisms and when I'm on my own. In fact, I see angels, Christian beings like Jesus or Mary, Muslim figures like Muhammad, other figures like Buddha, and more. I can recognize all of them because they show themselves as people have depicted them throughout my life. Jesus looks like the bearded, sandal- and robe-wearing hippie many of you studied in Sunday school, and Buddha looks fat, bald, and jolly. Whether this is how they actually look, or what they specifically wish to convey to me, I can't say. But that's how they reveal themselves to me.

The only major deity I haven't encountered is Satan himself, and it's unlikely he'll ever come to me since my Spirit Room is a one-way vortex, with everything that's low frequency going right out the door. If there's anything in the world that's low frequency, it's the Devil, so I can't imagine why he'd want to be anywhere near me or what I'm doing. Plus, honestly, I'm not even sure he exists. It just doesn't make sense that I've seen so many powerful, dark entities in my life, yet I've never seen Satan. After doing so many exorcisms, I've never had a single experience with an all-encompassing, pure low-frequency being. Could he exist? Sure. Maybe. But I've never encountered him, so I doubt it.

When holy beings show up, I don't even focus on their religious aspects. Instead, I concentrate on their energy, and all of them are very high frequency. Why? Because each and every one of them worked for good. They told us to be kind to each other and to love unconditionally, and it's mankind who misconstrued their lessons and used them to justify violent acts.

Different Higher Beings serve different purposes. For example, the Archangel Michael is a defensive player. At the beginning of an exorcism, I might ask him to ascend to my client's head to protect the crown chakra, where most of our spiritual downloading happens. I also might request that he protect their body and spirit during an exorcism, but not defend any negative energies or entities that don't belong there. I call in Michael more than any other religious being because it's really important to protect the body and spirit during an exorcism, and while other Higher Beings may do this, he's the one I'm most comfortable working with.

I also invite in the Angel Raphael when someone needs a lot of physical healing. His name means "Medicine of God" in Hebrew, and he's traditionally associated with bodily recuperation. He wants to make people well, and he does just that.

I don't just welcome in beings from the world's major religions, though. I also dig deep into history and mythology. I may see the Titans, whom the ancient Greeks worshipped. The Titans were believed to be the children of Gaia (the Earth) and Uranus (the sky), and I can recognize them by their huge size and enormous strength. They look massive, strong, and almost like they're chiseled out of granite, which is how they're frequently portrayed in artistic depictions of them. I might ask for help from pagan goddesses, Roman and Greek goddesses, beings from ancient African religions, Egyptian beings, or Native American spirits. I don't do this because I'm a scholar of the world's religions (I'm not). Nor do I sit for hours and decide who I want to have come to my aid. Instead, I can hear Spirit, and I can sense who wants to come in.

Most holy figures look exactly like you'd expect them to—or at least that's how they present themselves to me. The Archangel Michael has a very large stature, with massive wings, and he carries a sizable sword. The goddess Diana looks exactly as she appears in classical art: a proper Roman lady in the woods who just happens to be carrying a bow and arrow. Egyptian goddesses like Isis seem to be Egyptian, with well-defined eyes and short, stick-straight bangs and long hair. Athena appears fiercely intelligent. These beings take on their iconic looks, and my guess is that they do so because they want me to know exactly who they are, right away.

ANIMAL SPIRITS

I also see animal spirits, much like shamans do. These aren't actually animals, though; they're medicine spirits—often called "power animals"—and shamans request their help in healing. These figures reside in each person and act as guardian angels against illness, negative energy, and bad luck.

Animal spirits come in to help *me* rather than my clients during an exorcism. Essentially, they're not revealing something about a person, but rather assisting me in giving a person what I've discovered they need. For example, I sometimes see what shamans call a "jaguar spirit," which is a shapeshifter. One minute, he's a man, and the next minute, he's a jaguar. Shamans believe he assists people with reclaiming their power, and that's what I typically use him for, too. If I sense that a person is especially vulnerable to a bad situation, I might call in the jaguar.

If someone needs to attract something positive into their lives, I might ask "spider spirit" to weave its web to "catch" abundance or self-love. If it's revealed to me that someone needs freedom in their lives, I might welcome in a tiger or lion spirit, because that's what they represent.

With the exception of the jaguar spirit, who shapeshifts, all of these animal spirits appear clearly so that I can recognize them right away. Essentially, there aren't any great surprises when I see them. A lion spirit looks exactly like, you guessed it, a lion.

CHAPTER 9

The Exorcism Itself

W hen I meet a client, the first thing I do is congratu-
late them for even showing up to my house for an
exorcism. Getting to me was a major achievement.
Why? Because entities know they're going to be expelled long
before someone arrives in my Spirit Room, so often they'll cause
car trouble, convince a person to suddenly change their minds
about the appointment, or induce an illness that forces someone
to stay home.

Entities are notorious for disrupting technology, too, so I
always make people leave their cell phones and any electronic
devices outside the room. Sorry, no iPhones, iPads, or pagers
(do people even carry those anymore?), and I'd never allow any-

one to bring in an expensive camera, lest an entity smash the lens. I don't have any electronics in the room other than lights, nor will I ever. When entities enter a room, I've seen phones stop working for no reason and televisions go fuzzy, then black. And, forget it: I don't even try to do Skype conferences anymore.

I send my clients a list of guidelines before they come to me, so they arrive wearing simple, loose-fitting clothing, just like I've asked them to. Then I also make them take off their jewelry and their shoes so that they'll be as unadorned as possible. People don't realize that most jewelry—especially sentimental things that they've been given—carries intention and provides protection. For example, if you wear a wedding ring, there's deep meaning in that piece of jewelry. It signifies a profound, spiritual commitment to a life with another human being. People's intentions are remarkably strong. What we will, we create—like a marriage, represented by a wedding ring—and in some way that ring is protecting you from a life all alone. I don't like anything to interfere with the process of an exorcism, and jewelry might defend not just my client, but their entity as well.

Metal also carries a certain energy, which can disrupt an exorcism, so I always ask clients to take off any that they're wearing. As for shoes, removing them is just out of respect for Spirit.

I never ask anyone to take off their clothes, though my porn star clients are always ready to get naked. No surprise, they carry so much trauma in their genitals, and, without fail, they want to show me. But I do a lot of touching during an exorcism, and I just think it would be disruptive and weird—for you *and* for me—if my hands were all over your skin while I'm taking an entity out.

Next, I lower the lights and ask my clients to lie down on the queen bed that sits on the side of my Spirit Room. It's almost time—except for one important thing. Literally the minute before I begin an exorcism, I'll stand next to my client, lower my voice, and tell them: "Take note of your body and your spirit at this moment, because this is the last time in your entire life you will ever feel this way."

Many of my clients break down in tears at that moment. Why wouldn't they? More than anything, they hope I'm right. Way too many of them are just depleted from feeling so low for so long.

When the exorcism begins, I close my eyes and call in my Master Teachers. They're always with me, so it's natural to ask them for assistance. I won't necessarily use them to take out my client's entities—I mainly utilize other Higher Beings for that—but they reassure me and bolster me up. And when things *really* get tough—like when a client is screaming, vomiting, or crying out more than I feel they should, or if I'm exceedingly weak, tired, or nauseated—I can call on them, and they'll take the reins.

Next, I read the energy in the room, feeling where the high- and low-frequency areas exist. I need to bring in the high energy and push out the low, so I might move my arms around a lot, like I'm stirring the air. I circle a client's body, often speaking to the entity.

"I'm aware of you," I might say. "I know you're here." Then I'll get tough and give it a warning. "This is the last time you're going to be allowed to stay in this person."

I work closely with a client's body and spirit, speaking directly to them, asking them to work with me. I may put my hands on certain parts of a client's body, then pull energy and specific entities out, but that's really the only time I target and manipulate individual entities. Typically, I focus on the *whole* body and spirit system.

I might use a noisemaker (typically a shamanic-style tool like a rainmaker, rattle, singing bowl, or chimes) to agitate the energy in the room, too. Then, I stare into my client's body to see where the site of their trauma lies. As I move my hands down their sternum, over their chest, and slowly toward their belly, scanning for areas that feel and look dark, I'll start to feel nausea washing over me. Why? Because at this point I'm so deeply in touch with my client's body that, when they're infected with something malevolent, I feel like I am, too. The moment I feel sick is when I know I've hit the spot. As I look down, I'll see what looks like an oil spill or a small black cloud.

Finally, after I get a sense of the trauma I'm dealing with, I call in the Higher Beings who seem like they can best handle the situation. I need them not just to give me insight into what my client is suffering from, but also to face up to the entities who'll be repelled by their superhigh energy. It's sort of an indirect relationship; they're not familiar with me, but they know my client and have their best interests at heart, so they trust me. They'll give me information that I'd otherwise have no way of knowing. The Celtic woman I mentioned before might show up out of nowhere, or I might sense that I need the help of an angel who's assisted me in my last five exorcisms. If a client's come to me because of a trauma related to a deceased friend or family member, that person might enter, too. Every exorcism is different. But I never work alone, and I never follow a script.

Sometimes, though, I have no clue where the information I receive comes from. The fact that Spirit blurs is one of the many things that's so fascinating about it. I receive all kinds of signals about a situation or a person during an exorcism, but unless I ask, I'm flying blind. Often I'm too busy to even think about figuring it out, or it isn't relevant. But when I do ask, I always get the answer.

For example, I once had a client who was holding a lot of trauma in her wrists, which appeared as dark blockages under the skin, like an oil spill or a splotchy tattoo.

"Spirit," I asked, "why is there trauma there? Did something happen to this woman? She doesn't have any scars on her wrists."

Sure enough, Spirit revealed that my client had once attempted suicide by slashing her wrists. They were superficial cuts, though, and healed without leaving any scars. At the end of her exorcism, I told her what I saw and what I knew she'd done in the past, and she confirmed it.

Like I said before, entities are on high alert even before their host walks into my Spirit Room, and most are aware that I'm the one person who can destroy them. But I always give them a chance to leave of their own accord. If they decide not to, I start to pull in Spirit, which rushes high frequency through the body. This may sound silly, but think about those old commercials for drain cleaners, where a person pours something into a clog, and the cleaner coats as it goes down, then dislodges whatever's causing the problem, and, bingo! The water flows. It's totally satisfying to imagine, right? That's essentially what I'm doing. I'm exerting a positive pressure that forces out all that's negative.

Your body is like a clogged drain, and when you're stuffed up, you can't use it or your spirit to its full potential.

I frequently see celebrity clients—musicians, in particular—who complain that they've hit a creative rut.

"I'm having trouble producing anything," they might say. "I can't come up with anything new. It's like I'm blocked."

"You absolutely are," I always respond. "You have forty years of trauma, pain, drug use, and sexual dysfunction inside of you. You need to clean it out."

Within a few days of an exorcism, these musicians feel like they can breathe again. And, frequently, the next thing they write is an extraordinary hit.

◎

Oftentimes people wonder just what kind of role deceased relatives play in an exorcism. To explain that, I'll turn to my friend Teddy, whose exorcism I did about three years ago. To this day, his remains one of the most powerful, intimate exorcisms I've ever performed, and Teddy's recovery has been nothing short of miraculous. But I couldn't have done it without help in the form of his dead uncle. I'll let Teddy explain everything in his own words.

TEDDY

I met Rachel through my work in gaming marketing. Rachel's well-known in the gaming world, so we connected and became good friends. Pretty soon after we got close, Rachel told me that she could sense that something was off with me. I knew what she did on the side, so she urged me to stop by for an exorcism. I initially resisted, but she poked and prodded, and eventually, I gave in.

It's worth mentioning that I'm transgender, so I've been through a lot in my life. If you can believe it, though, the things that I'd been dealing with since I was a kid went way beyond that.

I was molested by my grandfather when I was young. I told my mom—who was only a teenager when I was born—about it, and she took the issue all the way to court. She protected me from my grandfather from the first moment on. But I was so traumatized by the abuse that I blocked it out for years. As an adult, I asked my mom whether it had really happened, and she was clear. "Yes, it happened, absolutely," she said.

I reconnected with my grandfather before he died, and we made peace as best we could, but I couldn't shake the guilt and confusion I carried around about the whole situation. Even though I knew, for sure, that he'd wronged me, I still felt bad. Maybe it had been my fault? Maybe I shouldn't have said anything?

Before I met Rachel, my life had become a mess. I was superpromiscuous, I did tons and tons of drugs, and I put myself into terrible, dangerous situations. I rarely had fun during any of it, and I became a walking, talking basket case radiating the bad vibes that I'd pick up from random strangers. I felt dragged down romantically, was struggling at work, and was anxious constantly. I had a big, black fog around me all the time, and every time I tried to move forward, I felt like there were roadblocks in front of me. Yet I couldn't put my finger on why—or do anything to undo it.

Then, I went to see Rachel. When I walked into her

Spirit Room, she asked me to lie down on a bed. I closed my eyes, and soon I entered an almost meditative space. As she burned herbs and started speaking, I felt protected. I was half out of it, but I still noticed that she was calling in Guides for herself and for me. One, in particular, was my beloved uncle, who was my mom's best friend.

My uncle had died of AIDS years before, but he'd always shown up in my dreams. When he did, I felt as safe as I did in Rachel's Spirit Room. He was my gay guardian angel, and I'd always suspected that what he did for me wasn't all in my head. Rachel confirmed it.

"He's been watching over you," she said. "He's protected you from contracting HIV, which you've been exposed to twice."

For the next ninety minutes, Rachel didn't just speak with my uncle; she also called in other spirits, walking me through each one. She's not a medium, but she can see things, and as she described these beings and how they related to me, part of me thought, *Has she been secretly watching me my entire life?* I started to feel this crazy energy running through my body, and I realized that I wasn't a passive party to what was happening to me. Instead, Rachel and I were fighting this thing together, and it was ultimately up to me to use my energy to expel it.

When everything was said and done, I sat up, and Rachel walked me through how I'd feel over the next few days. She told me what I should and shouldn't do.

"Don't drink, have sex, or eat anything that died unwillingly," she said. "And above all, rest, take care of yourself, and don't listen to your ego. Ignore anything bad that comes into your head."

For the next week, I felt like I'd been hit by a truck. My body was sore, like I had the flu, and I stayed home, rested, and drank lots of water. It took a while for my body and spirit to settle, but when it did, I understood right away that I had to confront the secret behavior I'd been engaging in. With Rachel, I'd gone on a journey that left me totally raw, yet lifted a huge weight off of me. I felt lighter. I knew from the bottom of my heart that I was a different person after seeing her.

Soon, I started to feel joy again, and I became careful of who I came in contact with. I started drinking less and stopped all the crazy promiscuous stuff. I kept anything and anyone who was toxic away from me. Even today, three years later, I feel like my life is forever changed for the better.

I use specific movements, light incense, or burn herbs that raise the frequency of the room and drive entities away. In a later chapter, I'll talk more about what these herbs and blends do, recommending which you can use on your own and how to mix them up right in the comfort of your own home. Many are far too dangerous for most people to have in their possession, but I'll outline what they are anyway.

Once I flood my client with high-frequency energy, the entities that are attached to them become immediately uncomfortable. The high-frequency energy is toxic to them, and they may start to fidget—spiritually and/or physically, depending on the person they've attached to—and this shifts the balance of their host's body and spirit. My client might become irritable, angry, hostile, or physically ill. As I mentioned before, it's not uncommon for people to vomit, sweat, twitch, shake, or just feel off. It's incredibly unnatural for a person's body energy to move and change so suddenly, so it's no wonder my clients don't feel right. But if they just bear with what I'm doing, pretty soon they will.

It's likely I'm feeling shitty, too. I frequently experience headaches, nausea, and aches and pains both during an exorcism and for a while after, and the more malevolent the entity, the worse off I am. I think the sickness I experience is as much about the force the entity releases as it is about the trauma the person went through to attract the entity. That is, if someone was raped multiple times by a family member, they're going to have a pretty sophisticated, dangerous entity with them, and I'm going to know it in every inch of my body. That trauma was awful, and I empathize with the person who endured it.

Finally, the time comes for me to destroy the entities. I don't truly "pull" an entity out. Instead, my clients' bodies expel them out of their physical and spiritual space. Lower-level entities, who cause less harm to a person, are always easier to remove. They're small and not as deep-rooted as the more dangerous entities, so they tend to flow right out once I begin my work. I like to imagine that they just can't fight against me, so that's why they hover outside of my client's body and then quickly dissipate. But if an entity has a symbiotic relationship with a person (as happens with a Trickster, when an individual is conscious of the connection with the entity but chooses to keep it anyway) or if it's been a part of their lives for years or even decades, it's going to fight me. It will resist leaving the body, cause both my client and me to feel very sick, and, if it has tentacles, clasp tighter.

The fact that I've created my space as a one-way vortex essentially holds the entity, and as the exorcism goes on, the entity begins to dissipate due to the high frequency I've helped generate. By the time the exorcism is complete, the entity has returned to smoke form. After that, it splits apart into tendrils, and then into nothingness. It's just *gone*.

What's Going On in My Head

I get all kinds of messages, visions, and sensations during an exorcism, and I have to try as hard as possible to divorce them from my ego. I want what I'm feeling to be about my client, not me. Exorcism is such personal work that this is not always easy, but I force myself to do it.

For example, during one recent exorcism I began receiving messages, mostly about blue velvet furniture, over and over and over. Now, I love blue velvet furniture. The chair I most like to sit in in my Spirit Room is a blue velvet egg chair. It's a cocoon that's so comfortable and warm that I named it "the Womb." I do all my work in that chair, and I feel connected to it in a way I've never felt about any other inanimate object.

When I started getting messages about blue velvet, I was initially confused. *What does my love of blue velvet have to do with this exorcism?* I thought. For a split second, I assumed what I was receiving had to be coming from my own ego. Then I came to my senses and realized it was exactly the opposite. This was an authentic communication right from Spirit, and it wasn't about me. It was about my client.

"I'm seeing something right now," I said. "I'm not exactly sure what it means yet, and I don't understand what it will mean to you, but what I'm visualizing is blue velvet furniture."

My client looked shocked. "Oh my God!" she squealed. "My grandmother had blue velvet furniture that she always covered in plastic because she didn't want it ruined."

That was all the confirmation I needed that what I was feeling wasn't from ego. My client's grandmother was one of her guiding ancestors and was with her at that moment. She wanted her to know that she was there, protecting her, during the exorcism. This kind of visitation isn't unusual; it's especially common with those who were extremely close to someone who passed, or those who were adopted who had biological parents or grandparents they didn't know who have crossed.

After my client's exorcism was over, I described her grandmother's spiritual presence to her, but I had to qualify it. I explained that her grandma was with her, guiding her, but that I didn't have a specific instruction from her. After all, I'm not a medium, so I can't say to a client, "Your grandmother wants you to know that she forgives you for climbing on her furniture when you were a kid. Also, she said she loves you very much." When I receive a message from someone's dearly departed loved one, it's just a validation that my connection with Spirit is authentic. It's proof that something from Spirit was there for my client during their exorcism. It's like the lollipop a doctor gives a kid when they're getting their shots; it doesn't heal an issue, but it helps make a difficult process easier to handle.

When It's All Said and Done

When an exorcism is over, I ask my clients to take stock of how they feel. One of the most frequent things I hear is that they sense a lightness, and that breathing, walking, and talking are suddenly easier. Oftentimes, a person will say to me, "I don't think I'll ever feel the way I did again," and I always agree. They may go out in the world and, a year later, experience a traumatic event that will lower their frequency, cause an entity to attach, and make them become depressed or anxious—but it will be a different kind of sensation. They'll experience a higher-minded depression, meaning that they'll have perspective. They'll be better able to deal with their emotions because they've gone through an exorcism and thus opened themselves up. Like Regina, they may come back for a tune-up, but the whole process will be easier.

I see life before and after an exorcism like a ladder. When a client first comes to see me, they may be at the bottom rung. On a scale of 1–13, with 13 being a Nirvana state that very, very few humans can reach, they're at a 3. Then, they get an exorcism, and it takes them to a 6. If they experience a trauma, they'll still be at a 6. Their spiritual potential stays exactly the same.

I'm always able to rid a person of their entities, but, unfortunately, I can't fix who they fundamentally are. There's a difference between what an entity does to you and what your personality is, so if you've been insecure since birth, that's not going to go away. If you're an asshole because it gets things done—or you just *love* being that way—you're going to be one until you decide to become something else. I can take out whatever amplifies your negative traits, but I can't change your character.

Three Days to Heal

Right before a client walks out the door, I ask them to sit down so I can talk with them.

"Look," I say, "for the next three days, you're going to be incredibly raw and vulnerable. Your spirit will be an open wound, and it has to scab up and heal over. Your body and spirit will still be purging the last of your traumas and your old low frequency, and anything that was being masked by the entity is going to bubble up to the surface."

Sounds a little scary, right? Honestly, it can be, but it doesn't *have* to be. Every client feels physically and emotionally different after an exorcism. Some people have flu-like symptoms, while others throw up for days. Some experience a lot of emotional peaks and valleys, and others suddenly remember things—good and bad—that they've repressed for years. On the flip side, though, some of my clients immediately come up with brilliant new ideas or visions, or have high-minded thoughts out of nowhere.

In the three days after an exorcism, my clients need to be cautious, and I explain exactly what this means. Because they're so energetically open—in such a vastly different way than they've been before—they're like a light in the dark to entities who want to attach to them. During that time, more layers of repressed trauma surface in an attempt to release from the body and spirit. The person holding them is deeply vulnerable. That's why they have to combat every negative thought that comes into their head.

"In the next three days," I'll explain, "you might hear a voice telling you to do something completely random, and sometimes violent. You might see an old woman crossing the street, and suddenly you'll be compelled to hit her with your car."

This out-of-nowhere inclination comes entirely from new entities who are trying to attach—and I tell clients to raise their frequency *immediately* to make it stop.

How? The answer couldn't be simpler. The client just has to be strong enough to say, "Fuck off." I want my clients to really *feel* what they're saying, so they should repeat it—loudly. "This isn't me, and you need to *fuck off!*" When a person talks to a new entity like that, they immediately become more powerful than it is, raising their frequency and sending it away before it can attach.

I also instruct my clients to take care of themselves. They shouldn't judge or overanalyze their emotions, and they should never be defensive or self-deprecating. They should get lots of sleep, drink plenty of water, avoid cigarettes, drugs, and alcohol, and eat a vegan diet—if possible. As I told Teddy, nothing should go into a client's body that has died in pain, as most slaughtered animals have. The reason is due to low frequency and vibration. During an exorcism, I send nothing but high frequency through the body in a very fast, very serious way, so to then go eat something with exactly the opposite energy level would lower the body and spirit's frequency. This is *not* something you want to do while you're in a vulnerable place. Finally, a person fresh off an exorcism should lie low and pamper themselves. Pedicures, long baths, and days off from work are all on the table.

Oddly, the three days after an exorcism can be a time of grieving. When a client relives a host of memories, experiences newly bubbled-up emotions, pain, or illness, they can go through feelings of isolation, as if they've just lost someone or something. They may even have dreams about their entities, and, trust me, these nightmares can be very frightening. I often have clients report that they've fallen asleep and heard a voice say, "I'm not gone," or "You didn't get all of me." That's an entity's way of trying to get in, so the person immediately needs to shout, "Fuck off!"

Don't think for a minute that this is the same entity that individual had before. It isn't. I destroyed the old entity fair and square. These are new entities, and they're attracted to a person who's energetically open. They'll say or do anything to invade them when they're at their most vulnerable.

I've only seen a few people leave an exorcism not feeling raw, and these were individuals who already vibrate at a high level. They'd been working on themselves for a very, very long time, bringing themselves to a place of high-mindedness, and they came to me 100 percent ready to release something very specific. It's like they'd already lost 200 pounds through diet and exercise, and I was the plastic surgeon who shaved off the last few stubborn ones they couldn't shake.

I don't always hear from clients after they walk out of my Spirit Room, but I always maintain intense hope for them. If I didn't, I couldn't perform this job. I have to remain optimistic so I can keep myself in the healthy mind-state I've worked hard to reach. I want to make a difference in the world, so I have to keep going, and keep my spirit strong.

Emergency Exorcisms

Most of the people who know about my gift are sympathetic to the erratic schedule that comes with my odd side job. My best friends understand that even if we schedule dinner weeks in advance, I may have to duck out before dessert. And vacations? Those are usually last-minute trips alone to the mineral springs in California wine country so I can soak my exhaustion away in a thermal bath and drink wine in peace and quiet. Life and people tend to adjust to what I do. But that doesn't make it any less awkward when I have to cancel an important meeting.

"I'm so sorry," I might say to a filmmaker whose script I'm writing, "but this superimportant actress, who's in the middle of a crazy production schedule, has been having night terrors, and the director's going to have to cancel the shoot if she doesn't get some sleep."

"And . . . what does this have to do with me?" comes the reply.

"Well, she's got an entity, and I need to exorcise it during the time we were supposed to have a meeting."

Believe me, this kind of conversation has been met with total, you-could-hear-a-pin-drop silence on the other end of the line. But what can I do? Somebody in a do-or-die situation needs an exorcism, and I'm the only person who can help.

There are only a few situations that'll make me stop everything I'm doing and rush back to my Spirit Room. Most exorcisms aren't emergencies, but a few are, and they typically don't deal with the type of entity I'll be battling, but instead the person who has it.

As I mentioned before, I *always* consider a child an emergency. Children are the closest beings in the world to Spirit, which gives them unadulterated innocence. Seeing that purity disturbed isn't just troubling, it's downright wrong. Plus, kids are blank slates who are too young to process trauma, so it's likely that they'll be significantly more affected than older people by entities. It's best to remove these forces as soon as possible.

I've performed exorcisms on children as young as two and three. Trust me, what these entities did to these beautiful little people was terrible. Not only were they emotionally stunted— not talking, acting withdrawn, or behaving oddly—but some even experienced physical trauma from the entity, like the child I talked about in the introduction. I saw strange words written in a tattoo-like fashion on one little girl. I witnessed unexplained cuts on a small boy's arms and legs, and bruises in private places on his body. Seeing these physical traumas upsets me deeply, and I always want to stop them immediately.

My youngest exorcism was on a girl who hadn't even turned two. Her parents were drug addicts, and her grandmother had taken custody of her when they were deemed by the court to be unfit. But before a formal transfer had taken place, the neglect was at its worst. Even with constant visits from her grandmother, who did her best to help a bad situation, the baby spent several months not being fed enough, sleeping in filthy conditions, and being ignored by her mom and dad. When the grandmother got custody, she took the baby to several doctors, but she still didn't put on weight or sleep through the night, and she spent most days crying.

"My neighbor said you might be able to help, so here we are," the grandmother said when she brought the baby to me. "You're my last hope."

We talked about what the girl had been going through, so her trauma was obvious. I didn't need her Guides to tell me much. But when her exorcism began, I discovered something much more complex: a Wraith, connected to sexual abuse that had happened years before the girl was born to a relative of hers, had passed through her spiritual DNA and attached to her. I call that a lineage connection, and the pain the entity had caused was being amplified by a Clive. When I exorcised the Clive and cut the lineage connection, both entities dissipated into smoke before my eyes.

The baby started sleeping through the night almost immediately. Within a month, she put on five pounds.

If I get a call from an old person, I also drop everything I'm doing and tell them to come immediately. This is not because I'm some sort of dark sage; I'm not peering into my crystal ball visualizing their imminent death, and what will happen to these elderly folks if they pass away covered with entities. I treat the elderly as I do children because the way their bodies process a possession isn't all that different. Think about how old people handle the teeniest, tiniest viruses like the common cold. They can get the sniffles, start to cough, go to bed feeling terrible, wake up with pneumonia, and then pass away quickly. It's similar with entities.

Most old people with entities have had them for years. I don't mean five or ten years, either. I'm talking *decades*. By the time an old person seeks my help, they're so used to the negative effects they don't realize it's possible to feel different. They may also suffer from physical ailments that they think are just the products of the passage of time. What they don't know is that their aches, pains, and diseases are actually because of entities, or at least are being made worse due to their being plagued.

The oldest client I ever exorcised was a ninety-five-year-old woman, and hers was a very complicated case. She was deeply depressed and had begun hearing voices. Her doctors were mystified; brain scans didn't show anything like dementia or Alzheimer's, which they assumed would cause these delusions. At the urging of her daughter, she finally decided that she didn't want to live her few precious remaining years on this earth in such pain.

"I've been through enough in ninety-five years," she told me. "It's time to try something new."

How could I dispute that? This lovely woman had an entity that was causing her health to decline steadily. It was taking too much out of her, and a medical doctor couldn't fix that.

When I brought her into my Spirit Room and asked her to lie down, I could see the site of her trauma with my own two eyes. What looked like ink blots lay at the base of her spine and deep in her core. Around them, I saw her entity. It was a Trickster, and it had clearly been attached to her for years and years because the feeling of malevolence surrounding it was much, much higher than your average Trickster.

The placement of the trauma makes sense, I thought. *The older a Trickster is and the longer you've had it, the more you stuff the trauma down, deep into your center.*

Like other Ancient Tricksters, it looked frail, decrepit, and almost paper-thin. It hovered outside the body but had tentacles that reached deep within my client. It had wispy hair and was ghostlike, like the figure in Munch's *The Scream.*

I could sense that it had kept my client in a cycle of self-deprecation. After losing many of her loved ones during childhood, and after living through World War II, Korea, Vietnam, and the Iraq War—all of which had stolen away people she loved—she felt defeated. She no longer saw the value in being alive.

She's in need of love and nurturing, I realized. Understanding that my client was a devoted Catholic, I decided to call in the most motherly Higher Being I know: the Virgin Mary.

With Mother Mary's assistance, we removed the Trickster after an hour or so of hard work. Then my client looked at me happily.

"I feel better already."

I told her and her daughter—who'd been waiting nervously in the next room—that her mother should take extraspecial care of herself for the next three days. I trust that she did so because I never heard from her again, and she promised to follow up if she had any issues. Even if she's passed, I'm comforted that her last years on earth were probably better than the decades before.

The last type of person I consider an emergency case is someone who's on the brink of doing something negative or destructive that will hurt both themselves and the world. I've never had a client who had his finger on the red button—or anything close to that—but I have seen musicians who had to perform the next day, but couldn't remember a single note; actors who kept stumbling in rehearsals and needed to pull themselves together before a shoot; and politicians who had an upcoming debate and realized that they just couldn't go through with it without my help.

I have clients who are on the verge of injuring themselves or others, or committing suicide. Clients—or their friends or relatives—will call in desperation, and tell me through tears that "She's going to kill herself tonight if she doesn't get help." The threat of that type of violence is the worst aspect of my job. I'm happy to face ten low-level entities for every one that's pushing an angry person toward hitting their spouse, or making a depressed person contemplate putting themselves out of their misery. In that situation, no amount of love, care, or medicine is going to help them. The entity they have is pushing that person toward misery or a horrible decision, and as long as they're willing, I'll get involved right away.

Remote Exorcisms

I try to never perform remote exorcisms. I did my first real exorcism—if you can call it that since it was so amateur—when I was outside and my boyfriend was inside, and it barely worked. I decided after that experience that if I couldn't see the blocks in a person with my own eyes, if I couldn't physically be there to pull out the entity, it wasn't worth my time—or my client's.

Now that I'm a little more seasoned, I do make exceptions. Remote exorcisms are extremely rare, and I've only done a handful of them because the circumstances surrounding them had to be extreme. My rule is: My future client doesn't have to be on the verge of death, but they should be physically incapable of coming to me. They have to be sick, bedridden, or so possessed that leaving their space would be seriously dangerous to their health or the safety of others.

The one thing that makes a remote exorcism easier is if I can get my hands on an object belonging to my client. And, it cannot be any random possession; it needs to be something that really speaks to and about the person, something deeply connected to their heart, mind, and spirit. I won't work with a ratty old T-shirt, for example. I need their writings, precious photographs, wedding ring, beloved locket, or something near and dear to them.

Just recently, I did a remote exorcism on someone who hadn't left his house for months. He was middle-aged and otherwise healthy, but he'd become catatonic and confined to his bed after losing the ability to walk. He looked like he'd aged twenty years, and he had a cough that lingered no matter how much medicine he took. His health issues had spiraled out of control so fast that his loved ones worried that he was dying. Getting him out of his house just wasn't in the cards, and there was no way I'd be able to talk face-to-face or on the phone with him.

When his wife called me, I asked her whether he had a personal object that I could use for the exorcism.

"It could be anything that's important to him," I said. "It just has to speak to who he is. It has to have him *in* it in some way."

"His artwork," she said without even pausing.

That was a perfect idea. My client had been a prolific artist all his life, and everything he drew seemed like it came straight from the heart. I realized I didn't need the originals, so I picked up a handful of prints from his wife and returned with them to my Spirit Room. I set all my equipment up just as if he were there, and I even put his artwork on the same bed where I ask my clients to rest. Then I did what I always do: called in the Higher Beings, channeled the energy I could feel coming from the prints, mixed and burned herb blends, and circled the bed in very specific intervals of time.

Believe me, it was a challenge, but eventually I felt the frequency of the room shift. I saw the blocks in my client's paintings, and as I lifted my arms I sensed the entity's low frequency close by, but not in my space. Pretty soon, I pulled the entity—a particularly potent female Wraith—into the room with me and noticed that she was attached to one print. Judging from how long my client had been sick and how old his paintings were, I knew the Wraith had been with him for about twenty years. Recently, she'd grown rapidly, becoming stronger and stronger as my client became sicker.

The exorcism took over an hour, and I was exhausted by the end of it, but I got rid of the vicious entity. I saw her lift right out of my client's painting, then dissipate in front of me.

That night, I decided I needed to get rid of this man's prints. It wasn't that the entity was in them—I'd seen her destroyed—it was because the art was a portal for the entity, and they were a site of extreme low frequency because of it. They were as raw and open as my client was going to be for the next few days. I decided I should burn the prints in the fire pit in my backyard, so I gathered some firewood and newspaper, laid down some kindling, and built a proper bonfire. The flames were just getting going when I threw my client's paintings on top of them.

Within seconds, I heard a loud *pop*! It wasn't like popcorn in a kettle, though; it was as if all the collective energy in the bonfire gathered together and decided to snap. I jumped back, just narrowly missing getting scorched. Here's the crazy thing. The flames from my little bonfire were four or five feet long—and they had come at me horizontally, like a bullet train at high speed.

"Oh my God! They're like . . . hands," said one of my friends, who'd decided to join me.

Sure enough, the flames didn't look like tongues of fire. They were massive mitts, and they clearly wanted to engulf me in a fiery hug.

I wasn't expecting to hear from my client's wife ever again, but a few days after the exorcism, she called me.

"He just left the house for a meeting," she said. "It's unbelievable. He actually looks healthy again. And he's walking."

I didn't tell her about the fire. All I cared about was that my client was well and back to his normal self, and that I'd done my job.

CHAPTER 10

Entities and Religion

'd be selling you—and this book—short if I didn't offer more discussion on how what I do intersects with religion. After all, it's a question I'm asked constantly.

I'm not a religious scholar by any stretch, but I do know that almost all religions have notions of demons, and they talk about them in their texts. Religious exorcisms have been performed throughout history, and many have been successful. If you go back as far as ancient Sumer, you can read about entities. One of the four holy books of Hinduism, called the Atharva Veda, describes the means of exorcism, which involve rituals, series of utterances, and a recitation of names. In Islam, exorcisms are actually considered a branch of alternative medicine. In Judaism, a rabbi who's mastered Kabbalah can perform an exorcism using ten men as helpers, reading Psalm 91 all together three times, and blowing a ram's horn.

I think this is wonderful. Like I said, I have absolutely nothing against any religion, and I actively seek guidance from all kinds of religious figures in so many of the exorcisms I do. But, honestly, I've never met a priest who *sees* entities the way I do. To clarify, I mean that while some Catholic priests have spent years training to do Catholic exorcisms—and then decades performing them—I don't think they've actually seen an entity with their own two eyes.

Why do I say this? Because a few years ago, a potential client asked me to be her wing woman while she visited a priest to discuss her possible exorcism, and I watched him dismiss her, even though she was clearly possessed.

This woman wanted to cover all her bases, so she'd consulted with me, then decided to seek the counsel of the church. We were both allowed only a small window of time with the priest, but as we sat with him, he asked her a laundry list of questions about how she was feeling, and the things that had happened to her in the previous few months.

His questions sounded like they were straight out of a manual called *Possession 101*. I can't remember them exactly, but I recall that most were about whether she'd consulted with doctors and psychotherapists. They were purely diagnostic, and there was no creativity, no nuance, and nothing that was specific to her situation. The priest just checked off her symptoms, then announced that she didn't meet the criteria for a church exorcism. He was 100 percent focused on whether or not my friend's symptoms matched up with what the church considered a possession. Not only that, but it was as if he wanted her to *prove* her case.

I didn't need proof. I could see this woman's Wraith as sure as the nose on her face. Nothing this priest did, said, or asked implied that he could, too. If he could sense entities—like I can—he wouldn't need a checklist, would he?

Religious Visitations

I wasn't raised religious, nor have I ever moved in circles where lots of people go to church or temple, talk about God, or even think about religion much at all. Because of that, I honestly wasn't aware of who Jesus was till I was well into elementary school. I never realized he—or really any other religious figure—was a driving force in millions of people's lives.

I just knew there was a man named Jesus who visited me sometimes at night. He started coming to me around the same time entities did, and I realized, without a doubt, that he was good. He didn't look like the white, bearded hippie with way-cool sandals you see in some paintings, though that's how he appears to me now. Instead, he was this *being* with a high-frequency glow. I felt good around him. He was powerful, but in a positive way. I knew he had no intention of ever hurting me.

Jesus wasn't the only religious figure who visited me when I was a kid. I saw angels, Mary, Muhammad, prophets, gods and goddesses, and other Higher Beings from old and new religions around the world. They never stayed long—but it was clear they wanted me to know they were there. And it always felt nice. I immediately had an affinity for these beings, and each and every time they came to me, I felt blessed.

I still do. Not only do these religious figures visit me during exorcisms, but I often see them in my bedroom at night, or while I'm writing in my Spirit Room. I know that they're Higher Beings, and because of that, they're inherently good. That's why I don't feel the slightest bit of inclination toward any religion. Each of them, via their figureheads, imparts positive ideas, so I could never choose one over the other. There's no right and wrong with any of them.

Now that my spiritual awareness is high, I've come to believe that I see religious figures because they want me to pass on a message to the rest of the world. The news is this: People often think that different religions and religious figures are at odds with each other, but that's not the case. At their core, each belief system wants us to be kind to one another, to treat each other well, and to work together to better humanity.

I'm constantly dismayed when I see how people have used religion to start wars, persecute, divide, and kill people. Don't they realize that it was man, not Jesus or Muhammad, who wrote all the books that laid out so many oppressive rules and laws? Don't they understand that the struggles on Earth have been created by man, but the beauty that comes from Spirit is great? And that if we tapped into Spirit regularly, we'd all be *so* much happier?

Absolutely. We'd also be able to ward off the worst entities imaginable, like the ones I encountered in the next two chapters.

CHAPTER 11

The Slaughterhouse Collector

Remember Jen and Sylvia Soska from the twin exorcism I performed in July 2016? Together, they host a game show called *Hellevator* for the Game Show Network and the highly regarded horror production company Blumhouse. The show is a horror-themed team challenge based around a central legend, with a gruesome, troubled character—such as a murderer, rapist, or serial killer—as the focus of each episode. The show is as much a mental contest as a scare-the-hell-out-of-you psychological test. By the end of each challenge, some contestants are covered in blood, some have been locked alone in a dark room, and others have been chased by cloaked figures wrapped in chains. At the end of the season, one team goes home $50,000 richer having outlasted and outsmarted all the other contestants.

Each episode is filmed in a warehouse in downtown LA, which I would guess was built around the 1920s. From the outside, it looks like the perfect location for a horror series because it's cavernous, bare bones, cold, and has dark levels connected by an elevator that seems like it might plummet straight to the basement at any moment. But the backstory of the building is far more fear inducing than what appears on-screen: for most of its history, this warehouse was a slaughterhouse. And for a brief window of time, it became a *human* slaughterhouse for an organized crime ring.

Jen and Sylvia had a bad feeling the second they walked into the space, but they went forward with the producer and director's plan to book it. After all, isn't a terrifying building with a dark, twisted history a dream-come-true location for a horror-themed game show? Still, the twins are superstitious, unfailingly cautious, and very Catholic, so they decided to have the set blessed by a priest before the cameras started rolling. They even decided to carry their own white sage—which people, including myself, use to elevate the energy in a space—every day during filming for protection.

Unfortunately, their precautions were for naught. White sage is really nice for making a space feel happy, but it's no match for an entity, and this warehouse was a dark place with a bad attachment. While they were filming the first season, thirty-eight cast and crew members were hospitalized—all in a matter of days—with what seemed like food poisoning. But when each of them was tested for what had made them ill, they received thirty-eight different results, none related to craft services.

The misfortune continued. Several crew members were injured on set, cameras stopped working, and every day in almost every room, something structural would break down.

Midway through the second season, soon after we first met, the twins invited me out for dinner, and Sylvia explained what was happening.

"Can you tune into spaces if you're not there? I mean, can you figure out what's going on with people or things even if you're not right there with them?"

"Sure," I said. "If I really try, I can definitely do that."

"Because there's a lot of weird shit going on where we film, and I think it's because the building used to be a slaughterhouse."

"And then the mob ran it after that," Jen added. "Then, it became a set, and—"

I interrupted her midsentence because she didn't need to go on. "Slaughterhouse" was red flag number one. If someone or something has been killed against its will, chances are its soul is trapped in the same location, and that's prime real estate for a malevolent entity—like a Collector—to attach and feed.

"When everyone started getting sick," Jen went on, "we asked one of our producers, Edward, who's also a medium, to look around. He went down to the basement and saw a ghost woman, with her fingers cut off. She was screaming for people to get out."

"Then he said he saw a man in the corner, who tried to grab him. When Edward tried to run, he couldn't find his way out," added Sylvia. "Now he refuses to come back. I don't blame him."

I knew what they were about to ask. *If it's an entity that's causing all of this*, I thought, *there's something I can do. If this only has to do with dead people, though, this one is out of my hands.*

Jen interrupted my thinking. "What does this feel like to you?"

"Well, I sense that it's probably an entity. But I have to go inside to be sure."

I spent the next few days waiting for Jen and Sylvia to brief their production company about why they'd have to halt filming. Some of the execs rolled their eyes when they were told that an exorcist was coming in to check things out—but not too much. We all work in the horror industry, in Los Angeles, after all. It wasn't so far-fetched.

When I got word from Jen and Sylvia I went into my Spirit Room and pulled together my "travel kit." I made what I call a blood vinegar, which is a combination of fermented red wine, specialized herbs, red wine vinegar, and a few drops of my own blood. The blood is to combat a sacrifice with a sacrifice, so I pricked my finger and let a few drops fall into a spray bottle, which I planned to use to clean the walls, floor, and ceiling. I don't use this blend in every exorcism—just for Realm Walkers and Collectors because they require something especially potent. Blood vinegar is that. It immediately and forcefully cleans the energy of an area.

I also gathered together a few herbs like wolfsbane and blue lotus, which I only use for exceptionally powerful exorcisms. I combined the herbs into blends that I planned to burn, loaded up my car, and drove toward the old slaughterhouse.

As I got closer and closer to the building, I instantly sensed a darkness. *Yep,* I thought. *There's an entity here. This sure as hell isn't a haunting.*

I'm a no-nonsense woman, so I decided I'd head right to the basement as soon as I told my friends I'd arrived. Since it had been a slaughterhouse, I knew there would be tons of tiny rooms in the massive 13,000-square-foot space, places where refrigerators, furnaces, meat hooks, and God knows what else had been housed. Most rooms were separated by vast, empty spaces that I assume served as the gathering place for the poor cows awaiting their deaths.

As I walked down a set of metal stairs, I could feel the negative energy pooling in every molecule in the air. It was cold and empty, with a sense of violence and desperation. Even if I hadn't heard about the girl with the severed fingers or the man who'd grabbed poor Edward, I knew that that basement was a low-frequency cesspool.

"Here's where they bled out the slaughtered animals," Sylvia said as she pointed to an area near the meat locker. "They called it the bleeding room."

I walked inside and looked down. There was a drain in the middle of the floor that captured the blood from the cows who'd hung, dead, above it. I pulled off the grate to reveal a gaping hole, opened up my blood vinegar, and poured it into the earth below to cleanse it.

There are gallons of blood down there, I thought. *That's decades of sadness and pain for an entity to feed upon.*

Then, I began lighting the blends I'd brought along. As the dark room began to fill with smoke, I called in the Higher Beings and began to communicate with Spirit. I frequently work with the Egyptian goddesses, so I welcomed them, along with Lilith, a goddess with Hebrew and Sumerian roots, who's famous for her powerful dark energy. Archangel Michael was there for protection, and I called in Diana, the goddess of the hunt, to help me assist the dead animals.

Probably ten minutes passed, and then, suddenly, my vision cleared. Right in front of me I could see a dark cloud. It was hovering and barely swirling, and inside, there were shadowy forms. I could hardly make out faces, but I saw hooves, ears, and a tail here and there. Right away, I realized what they were: slaughtered cows, their mouths open as they screamed in silence.

Holy shit, I said to myself, *they're inside the biggest Collector I've ever seen.*

Inside that bleeding room, I found just what I'd suspected: a Collector had attached, gathered up the souls of the cows killed there, and was feeding off their suffering. The cows were in limbo, trapped in the same fear they'd had at the last moment of their lives.

Just then, a sharp voice cut through the dark and silence.

"Stop! Right now! You have to stop."

I turned and squinted. It was pitch-black except for my burning herbs, but I could just barely make out three masked men standing directly in front of me.

"You're from the crew, right?" I asked. All of the production crew on *Hellavator* doubled as actors, and they wore masks during filming to scare the contestants.

"Yes," one of them said, "you can't be in here doing this."

I never argue my way into an exorcism. It's not my space and it's not my place, and if someone wants to end an exorcism before it's reached its logical, spiritual conclusion, I can't stand in the way of that. Plus, I'd been interrupted before when I exorcised a building. I wasn't going to take it personally.

"Not a problem," I said, and I gathered my things and walked back up the rickety steps. When I couldn't find Jen and Sylvia, I decided to get back in my car and head home. After I buckled up, I texted them.

Hey. I left. Somebody on your crew kicked me out. I started and didn't get to finish, so I can't be responsible for what happens now.

It was true. When you disturb an entity, like I had, it goes on high alert. It knows that someone—specifically, me—is minutes away from killing it, and it's going to lash out. Jen, Sylvia, and everyone on the *Hellavator* set were in for trouble until I finished my work.

Jen finally called me an hour later.

"I can't believe someone kicked you out!" she said. "We had approval from everyone, every single person involved in this show. This is ridiculous."

"I don't know what to tell you," I said. "But I was told to go, and I do as I'm instructed. So just call me again when I can come back."

A few days later, Sylvia rang me up.

"You *have* to get back here as soon as possible. *Please.* It took us fourteen hours to shoot our last episode. Nothing worked: The electrical equipment. The audio equipment. Our audio was bleeding into rooms that it wasn't even linked up to. We lost so much footage. Then one of our girls fell, fractured her arm, and smashed her head. *Please* come back."

"I will, but who was it that sent me home?" I asked. "There were three guys, but one of them seemed like the boss."

"One of the crew. Strangely, he has no idea why he told you to leave. He can't explain what motivated him to even speak to you."

He might not have known, but I did. The most malevolent Collector I'd ever encountered had taken control of him that afternoon, and it had coerced him to drive me out.

The next day, I once again packed up my blood vinegar and blends, drove over to the slaughterhouse, and picked up where I'd left off. I'd already cleared the negative imprint from the bleeding room, so it was no longer emitting a negative frequency. But the rest of the basement was a different story; it was vibrating at such a low level that the entity was revolting. We could hear pipes cracking and squealing, footsteps in places we knew there weren't people, and there was a low, moaning hum echoing throughout the entire floor.

Despite that, Jen and Sylvia wanted to be with me as I worked. As you know, I usually don't allow anyone to join me during an exorcism, but Collectors are a little different than most entities. They're attached to the space, so the possibility of them attaching to a person in the room is nil.

"You can hold the lantern while I do my thing," I said.

"Aren't you scared?" Jen asked.

"No." It was true. I knew what I was up against.

I'd spent about an hour earlier that week exorcising the bleeding room, but I hadn't closed up the space. On top of that, there were dozens of other rooms I hadn't even walked into, and I knew that the Collector had entered each of them. Finally, I could sense that the trapped souls of the cows were still hanging in the balance. A lot of horror movies had been shot down in that basement, so the cows' spirits had seen some terrible things: killings, decapitations, and gallons of blood. Since organized criminals later owned the warehouse, I suspected they'd done even worse. They'd murdered people for real, and God only knows how they'd done it. The poor spirits who'd lived in the Collector's version of purgatory had seen so much violence, not knowing most of it had been fake. They weren't yet able to pass back into Spirit because my exorcism the other day just hadn't done enough.

"Cows?" I called out as I put down my supplies, started lighting my blends, and summoned Hecate and the Archangel Michael. "You don't need to be scared. I know you saw so much, but most of it wasn't real. Your own murders weren't being reenacted. And if you did see something real, I'm going to remove it now."

Just then, Jen, Sylvia, and I heard high-pitched screams cut through the room.

"What the hell was that?" yelled Jen.

"It's all the neighborhood cats," I said after listening for a moment or two. "Relax. Animals are very sensitive during exorcisms. They're feeling the change in frequency."

Then the pipes in the room started dripping water.

"Rachel, what exactly is that?" Sylvia asked. "I'm scared out of my mind."

I knew no water had gone through the pipes in years, so it had to be a message of some kind. When I exorcise a Collector, the spirits who've been trapped in a space—much like the cows who were screaming in the bleeding room—usually try to send me signals. *If the mob used this room,* I realized, *these pipes were probably a way for them to get rid of bodies. They probably dissolved these dead people in acid, then sent them through the pipes.*

"There are trapped souls traveling through these pipes," I said. "They're trying to communicate with us. They want us to know what happened to them, so they're making the water drip."

Jen went pale and Sylvia looked like she was about to retch, but I kept on my task as I moved from room to room. LA was suffering through a horrible heat wave that week—it was well over 100 degrees outside—but the rooms were all ice cold. As I pulled a sweater around me, the air around me started to constrict. I approached a corner of the basement, moving slowly to rid the room of low-frequency energy, and I saw a figure in front of me. It was a man, in his midtwenties, with dark hair and a nice suit. He was crying, his shoulders slumped as he lifted his head. I began to speak with him.

"Are you okay?" I asked.

"No. I'm afraid to move on from this place," he answered. "I'm scared I'll go somewhere worse than this if I do."

"Rachel?" Sylvia yelled at me. "Who are you talking to? There's no one there."

"Sshh," I said. I knew I couldn't answer her right away. After all, the spirit I was speaking to was a dead mobster, and I was trying to reassure him that the entity who'd kept him locked in a basement for decades would soon be letting him go.

"Look," I explained, "it's going to be okay. You just need to come to grips with what you've done in life before you can pass back to Spirit. Can you do that?"

Judging by how upset he was, the man had obviously committed horrible crimes in his life. But as he wiped tears from his face and nodded his head slowly, he seemed remorseful. That would likely be enough to allow the entity to release him.

As my blends continued to burn, I could see that light had begun to seep into the basement. The air wasn't so constricted anymore, and as Jen, Sylvia, and I moved toward a room that had been used to store props like coffins, I could tell that the Collector was exiting the space, leaving a void we had to fill so another entity wouldn't come in.

This storage room had electrical cables hanging from the ceiling and piles of papers and boxes stacked in every corner. It was a mess, but you could feel how light the energy was there. It was a radical shift compared to what I'd felt an hour before. The sense of desperation we'd all encountered had lifted ever so slightly as the spirits of the cows, the murdered people in the pipes, and the dead mobster had finally been freed.

Then, suddenly, I heard Jen gasp.

"Oh my God!" she screamed. "One of the cables is tied into a noose!"

I looked to my left, and there was a perfectly tied noose hanging from the ceiling. This was no prop. No one except for Jen and Sylvia had been in the storage room in weeks.

I knew right away what the noose was doing there.

"It's okay," I explained. "Somebody probably hung themselves in this room, and they're giving us a message that their spirit has been released, too."

As the room continued getting warmer, and light flowed in, I knew we'd officially turned a page. The Collector was gone, the basement was returning to a stable, steady frequency, and my friends could return to work. I took about three hours to go back through the warehouse and close the space up, but I left no room untouched and no stone unturned. Then I walked back up the steps, went home, and fell into my bed.

I slept for ten hours straight. I'd done one hell of a tough job. *Hellavator* was now safe for as many seasons as it was destined to run, and there would be no freak accidents, screaming cats, leaky pipes, or nooses. The Collector was gone, and many, many souls had been freed to pass back into Spirit. One more little pocket of the universe was entity-free.

With every ounce of my being, I hope something similar happens during the next large-scale exorcism I might undertake.

CHAPTER 12

Exorcising the Cecil

I f the stars—and the red tape that rules Hollywood—align, I may soon face the most difficult, intense, and possibly life-threatening exorcism of my life. Almost all my interactions with Realm Walkers have centered around the people they've possessed, but this one is different. This incredibly malevolent entity has attached to one of the most infamous buildings in Los Angeles—and I've been tapped to do something about it.

In downtown LA there's a hotel formerly called the Cecil that's notorious for a string of unsolved murders and violent crimes that have occurred there. From the location, this is not surprising. The Cecil is just west of Skid Row, where about five to ten thousand homeless people live at any given time. In less than five square miles, the homeless are packed on the streets in sleeping bags, cardboard boxes, and tents. These poor people aren't drifters, either; they come to Skid Row, and they stay. The local government has done a lot of things over the years to try to clean up the area, including tearing down abandoned buildings where the homeless are squatting, issuing tickets, or even arresting people, but none of these methods have proven very successful.

About 20–25 percent of homeless people are estimated to be mentally ill, and entities prey upon them. Why? Because the mentally ill are often low frequency. These unfortunate souls don't have the mind set to view the world in a high-minded way. They're trapped in a prison of their own brains, constantly fighting against themselves, unable to make the rational or spiritual decisions that could better their lives. They're energetically open sores: the perfect target for entities. So if you see a homeless person standing on a street corner screaming to no one in particular, swatting at his head, or trying to speak with someone who's not there, it's likely that there *is* something there. It's an entity.

Over its almost one-hundred-year history, the Cecil has never risen above the Skid Row fray. Sadly, it would be difficult for the hotel to do so; it's right on Main Street, in the center of everything, so even though the lobby is an art deco masterpiece, the Cecil's always been a favorite of cash-strapped people who manage to pull together enough change for a cheap bed. At first, around the time of the Great Depression, it was a place where transients could stay while they looked for work. Years later, it became a single-room-occupancy hotel, and prostitutes and drug addicts moved in.

Unfortunately, being so low frequency, the Cecil's also attracted *much* worse.

In the 1950s and '60s, several people jumped from the hotel's highest floors to commit suicide. One landed on the hotel's marquee. Another fell on a pedestrian walking down the sidewalk, killing him instantly. In 1964, a retired telephone operator known for feeding the neighborhood pigeons was raped, stabbed, and strangled in her room. Then, in the 1980s, Richard Ramirez, the "Night Stalker," lived on the top floor during the time he terrorized Los Angeles by breaking into homes and killing thirteen women. In 1991, a man named Jack Unterweger lived in the Cecil and murdered three prostitutes.

The hotel was sold and renovated in 2007, and some of the floors were converted to a standard hotel, while others became a hostel, but that didn't stop the terrible acts from happening. In 2013, events reached a gruesome climax when the body of Elisa Lam, a twenty-one-year-old student from Canada, was found in the water tank on the top of the building. Elisa had been missing for nineteen days, and hotel employees only discovered her body when guests began complaining about brown, foul-tasting water coming out of their bathroom taps.

Elisa's death was eventually ruled an accidental drowning, but many unanswered questions remain. Elisa would have only been able to get to the roof via the fire escape or through a locked door that would have tripped an alarm when opened. She was also so tiny that there was no way she could have lifted the incredibly heavy cover lid of the water tank without help. Elisa was known to be bipolar, but she'd been taking her medication, and there were no other drugs in her system at the time of her death. She didn't leave a note, either, so it seems unlikely that she committed suicide. Finally, there was no sign of trauma on her body, so even if she was murdered, how could the killer have lifted the tank lid *and* forced her below the water without signs of a struggle on her body? The facts of the case are puzzling, to say the least.

But I think the biggest mystery comes from the last images of Elisa on the hotel's elevator camera. In the footage she seems to be hiding from someone or something and then arguing with them as she waves her hands in the air. Yet that person never shows up on the screen. Who—or what—was it?

I know the answer. I can see the truth from a mile away. The Cecil is, without a doubt, dominated by a Realm Walker.

How do I know this? Those who are aware of my work as an exorcist send me information about "unsolved mysteries" all of the time—like photographs, links to articles, and video footage. Time and time again the question will be asked: "Is this person possessed?" When the video of Elisa Lam's last moments on the elevator went public, a friend of mine sent it my way. Now, my friend wasn't the only person in the world to think that something was off about that video. If you google "Elisa Lam Cecil" and watch the footage, I'm pretty sure you'll think it's strange, too.

I sensed something very, very dark, deep down in my bones, the second I looked at the video. I could see a shadow on the film. Part of me thought it was a Collector, but since that's such a rare entity, I decided to sleep on it and take another look in the morning. Sure enough, when I woke up and logged on to my computer to watch the clip a second time, I could only draw one conclusion. The video of Elisa's last moments showed something bigger and more malevolent than a Collector. It was most definitely a Realm Walker.

How can I be sure it's not a Collector? Again, because Collectors only work on those who enter the space. A Realm Walker has a long range, and it can pull people in from outside a location. That's the main difference. They are much stronger, much smarter, and know how to lure.

I am now certain that every horrible thing that's happened at the Cecil since 1925, including the death of Elisa Lam, has been caused by a massive entity who has its grips on the building itself. I've now looked at hundreds of photos of the Cecil, and in each and every one, I can see a giant, dark cloud covering it. Even from an image online, I can sense the most malevolent energy I've ever felt in my life.

During all the years I've lived in LA, I've never been into the Cecil. My reasons have nothing to do with the neighborhood because Downtown has started to revitalize and is now a mecca for hipsters. The Cecil is doing its best to keep up, and it's once again undergoing what the management describes as a "seismic upgrade." But I won't be hanging out there. It's not that I don't think they'll do a wonderful job; it's just that I have no desire to experience the nastiness that dwells within.

Well, that's not the whole truth. . . . I haven't been to the Cecil because the Realm Walker that's in control of it knows who I am and what I do—and I am certain he wants me to stay the fuck away.

In late 2016, the Soska twins approached me about working on a documentary about the Cecil. I'd discussed with them my belief that there was an enormous entity there, and that for years I'd been considering approaching the management about exorcising it.

"What's stopping you?" the sisters asked. "In fact, we'll get permission for you. You exorcise the Cecil, and we'll film the whole thing."

I thought about it for a long time. *Would people think I was doing this just for publicity?* I wasn't. That hotel is dangerous, and it needs to be dealt with. Also, if I wanted publicity so badly, why have I been doing this job for years in secret? Instant fame is so easy these days. Just go on the Internet, post a picture of yourself half-naked, and you're a celebrity. That's not me. I've been offered reality series and have turned them down. I don't give a shit about fame. I have a higher calling.

I finally said yes to the Soskas, and that's when things really started to amp up.

Just a few days after I took them up on their offer, I was driving my car in LA—nowhere *near* the Cecil—and a white dove just fell from the sky. I wasn't on a busy street, so I decided to pull over and take a look at this bird. Other than the fact that it was dead, it looked young and normal, with no obvious signs of illness, blood, or injury. Even stranger, there were no trees nearby. The dove had just plummeted out of the clear blue sky, lifeless.

Yet it had an unmistakable energy signature—something I'd felt before. It matched the expansive, almost unbearable malevolence I sensed every time I saw photos of the Cecil. I felt hollow and cold, as if all the energy in the air around me were being sucked away. I knew right away the Realm Walker had killed the poor bird, and he was warning me to stay away—or he'd try to kill me, too.

The behavior of the homeless people near my home, the coffee shops I like to go to, and the large corporate office buildings where I sometimes take meetings for my day job has also started to change. As I've become invested in the documentary and the history of the Cecil, the transients I've always passed on the street have become increasingly more agitated. And there are more of them, and they're acting out. Just after Thanksgiving, I walked past a homeless man near my house. I went into a store, came out a few minutes later, and passed him again. Then I realized I'd left something behind, so I doubled back past him a third time. Suddenly, he jumped up from the ground, rushed toward me, got into my face, and started shrieking, "Fuck you! Fuck you!" He went from blasé to threatening in a matter of seconds, as if he'd been taken over by something. In fact, I knew he had. When he was near me, his energy matched what I'd felt when the dove landed in front of my car. He was plagued by the Realm Walker, and it wanted to scare me.

When word started to spread about our documentary, the same kinds of things began happening to the Soska twins. They were accosted by several homeless people who hurled insults at them—specifically about projects these people should have known nothing about, like our film. One man spat at them and yelled, "Don't go near that hotel!" When they tried to rush past him he lunged at them and screamed, "I'll kill you if you do!"

You're probably thinking, *Wait. If the Realm Walker lives in the Cecil, how the heck is he traveling across Los Angeles, killing innocent birds and attaching to homeless people?* That's what's so terrifying. What I've realized is that this ugly beast can possess several people at once. It can leave its chosen location—the Cecil—and migrate from one person to another in an effort to damage everything in its path *and* stop me from doing my job.

This entity is smarter and more sophisticated than any I've ever come across. I know I need to be more prepared for this exorcism than any I've done before. I've thought about visiting the Cecil to gather information, but I fear it would be too dangerous. I don't want the entity to learn too much about me because if he does, he could destroy me. I know I'll become too familiar to him, and he'll try to play on my weaknesses.

When I finally do enter the building, I need to be fully armed with my Spirit Guides, my blends, and a team of psychic warriors such as mediums and oracles, who'll help keep me from being distracted. If I don't have to tune in to, say, the dead people in the Cecil, I can concentrate solely on the entity.

All I can do is prepare myself for what lies ahead, whether my battle is tomorrow or years from now. I know I need to be as healthy and strong, both physically and mentally, as I've ever been in my life. I'm already doing the work: exercising, eating clean, sleeping well, meditating. My mind and body will need to be armed for battle, and I'm going to do everything I can to wage it as forcefully as I can.

Honestly, I have no clue what to expect other than the hardest day, or days, of my life. I don't know how, or if, it's going to change me—physically and spiritually—forever. Chances are good that the Realm Walker will cause me and my team physical harm. Some of us may become gravely ill and land in the hospital. We'll hear screams and insults, and have to duck from objects being thrown at us from all sides. It's even possible the whole building will come crashing down just from the sheer amount of energy rushing through the space.

I've come up with what I hope is a foolproof plan, though. I'll move through the building twice, starting on the roof and making my way down to the basement. On my first go-through, I'll work on pulling the entity out of the building, and on my second trip from top to bottom, I'll close up bad energy in the space by burning high-frequency herbs. At the end of an exorcism, a building is no different than a person; when you remove such a powerful entity, what's left behind is raw, open energy. It's space that's ripe for another entity to come back in, or, worse, for someone inside to get hurt, sick, or killed. The entity might inflict structural damage, so anything from broken pipes to live wires could crop up. Therefore, I have to close the building completely, even more carefully than I did after exorcising the Slaughter-house Collector.

I plan to take an all-female camera crew with me. Why? Because I know the Realm Walker absolutely hates women. Most of his victims have been female, and his particular skill is taking over men so that they can harm women. Having women with me will make the entity even more agitated. I'll prep my team beforehand, sitting down with them every night for at least two weeks, teaching them how to raise their frequency so they can walk into the building ready for battle, too. I also suspect that the homeless people who live around the hotel will try to attack us when we enter, so we'll sneak in via the service entrance, hope-fully undetected.

Since I haven't been in the Cecil, I know there are a lot of things I'll discover when I enter: just how the entity operates, what its weaknesses are, and how it will try to destroy me once I begin the exorcism.

Thankfully, I already know I'll win, because I understand how it originated. Sure, the Realm Walker comes from Spirit, like me, you, and every high and low being out there, but its origins are bigger and more complex. I've broken my rule of not do-ing research before an exorcism and studied hundreds of pictures of the Cecil online. In each one, I can sense, plain as day, that there's a massive vortex on the land where the hotel was built. I can't actually *see* it with my own two eyes, but I can feel its dark energy just by looking at photos. It's the most negative emptiness I've ever experienced; staring into it, it's like I'm floating in the darkest kind of negative space, gasping for my last breath.

It's clear that the vortex is sucking so much low-frequency energy into itself that it's become a sort of on-land black hole. It's a stationary hurricane, with the Cecil as its eye. In fact, I suspect that the hotel was built *specifically* to serve the purposes of the vortex. It wanted to draw vulnerable people toward it, make them stay, and destroy them.

The Realm Walker has sprung from this, and it's drawn negative energy from it for almost ninety years. It doesn't give a shit about who or what it's attached to and then fed off of; all it cares about is that it can control hundreds, even thousands of people, and then murder them rapidly. It killed Elisa Lam, it murdered the Night Stalker's victims, and it wants, more than anything, to destroy me.

I'm ready—or at least I think I am. I know how to kill the Cecil Realm Walker, and I've never failed in any other exorcism. Spirit's on my side.

CHAPTER 13

Bad Moons, Lost Souls, and Making Sense of Everything

My unique window into Spirit has exposed me to a lot that's ugly and downright scary. That's been true my whole life. I've learned to deal with it, though, so now I never tune out what's fearful. Never for a minute do I regret the gift I've been given. I process it and use it, and I haven't just learned important lessons, but I've also made the lives of my clients better.

Over the years, my psychic awareness has grown, and this has allowed me more access to the spiritual world. I haven't just seen more entities, but other beings as well. I've spent the last ten years trying to make sense of patterns, and what to do in situations beyond the normal exorcisms. Maybe you think this all sounds overwhelming, but I think it's the most exciting challenge I could face.

What Goes Bump in the Night

Sometimes, there's absolutely no pattern associated with how entities behave or when they appear. When I was a child, and well into my twenties, I was bombarded by entities at all hours, with no rhyme or reason. Sometimes, I suspected they did it simply to scare me. Other times, they wanted to attach to me.

I'm now a lot smarter, and much more experienced, and I've come to understand the patterns that entities follow with their visitations. For example, I've learned that entities are more active at night. Spirit has never told me why, and I certainly don't have any scientific explanation for it, but I have a sneaking suspicion it's because of lunar cycles. Think about it: if more women go into labor during the full moon, more people commit suicide then, and tidal patterns change as the moon waxes and wanes, doesn't it make sense that the Spirit world might open up with the moon, too? There's just something about night energy and the way the full moon makes you feel; it's full of wonder, and it opens you up, causing all your strengths, weaknesses, fears, and joys to bubble to the surface. You're more receptive and alive, and that's when entities spot you and try to come in. Again, this is all just my hunch and based entirely on my own personal experience and my work with clients, but I have noticed a pattern.

They May Not Be Out to Hurt You—But It Still Hurts

Now that you've learned about nighttime visitors like the Sandman or a Wraith, you likely assume that if an entity comes to you at night, it must have malicious intent. But this is not necessarily the case. Yes, the Wraith and the Sandman are the entities most active after the sun has set, but just because an entity visits then does not mean it intends to attach itself to you. In fact, it may just be passing through. This happens to me *all the time,* and I know from talking to clients that it's happened to them, too. Remember the Wraith I saw stretching herself over my boyfriend late one night? She wasn't looking to invade me or him; she just wanted to show herself. Entities can be cocky and like to show off—and this occurs especially after dark.

There's nothing I can do to prevent them from coming to me. I tried when I was a little girl, and I failed miserably *and* made myself deeply unhappy in the process, so I've learned resistance is futile. Instead, the best I can do is let go, accept that it is my role on this planet to see entities, and then focus all my energy on raising my frequency so that I can keep them from trying to attach to me in the wee hours when I'm asleep. To do this, before I go to bed, I ask Spirit for help, saying, "Please enter my body and spirit to protect me." Often I'll burn incense as well. I also wear protective jewelry, including a copper plate that hangs on a thick chain around my neck. It features three goddesses on it.

Even with all of this precaution, though, I never sleep well. My heightened awareness means that I never fully relax or regularly fall into a deep sleep like most people do, and this makes it hard for whoever might be sleeping over. I've heard so many times, "I'd love to see entities like you do," but trust me, you don't.

Bad Moons

Visitations are most concentrated during what I call Bad Moons. The name says it all: A Bad Moon is an intense negative occurrence that happens overnight and in regular intervals—not *quite* correlating with the lunar cycle, but instead about every six to eight weeks.

During Bad Moons, I'll get visitations from entities *all* night long. My entire house will become a place of heightened activity, with doors opening, cabinets slamming, and books falling off bookshelves. I'll hear screams, talking, and even whispers, coming from every room. The energy in my house feels heavy and dark, and everyone present is on edge—adrenaline high and poised for escape. My poor animals are especially sensitive during times like this, crawling into their crates or curling up at the end of my bed.

There's no sleep for the wicked during Bad Moons. In fact, I end up staying awake those nights to keep my frequency high and prevent them from attaching.

The crazy thing is that I feel the Bad Moon coming. About twenty minutes before a wave of entities shows up, my whole mood changes. I'll start to feel anxious, frightened, or sometimes even irate. It's like a tsunami is approaching, and I'm the lone elephant, standing on the beach with every hair on my body raised. I'll tense up, close my eyes, and try to prepare. Then the doors blow open, and the entities don't leave until the morning.

All night long, I fight them. I scream for the entities to leave me alone, burn herbs, make a mean blood vinegar, and think happy thoughts. But they just keep coming. . . .

I've tried to figure out exactly when Bad Moons happen, but so far I haven't been successful. Still, something in my gut tells me—and if there's anything I've learned from Spirit, it's that my gut is usually right—that Bad Moons are a way to regulate the universe. If I spend eight straight weeks destroying dark entities, the balance of the universe is off. One night of constant negativity is sort of like the universe's death throes, pooling all the world's low frequency into one place to torture me.

The Deceased and What They Bring

As I've mentioned, I often see dead people during exorcisms. These can be the recently deceased, who show up when they're connected to the trauma that led to the attachment. Sometimes I'll welcome ancestors, who have been secretly guiding individuals through their lives. But I also have the ability to see dead people outside of exorcisms, and often, they visit me whether I like it or not.

I never saw the dead when I was younger, and, in fact, I didn't fully tune in to that ability until about three or four years ago. I wasn't ready; I needed to accept my life as an exorcist first. Connecting with the deceased was not something I wanted. In fact, I actively avoided it. My opinion was: *I already see too much. I just can't take more.* It wasn't until I was really, truly ready to handle more than just entities that I let the dead in. Now I see them frequently.

I don't claim to be a medium, nor do I want to be. It's not

that I don't respect what they do—I have many friends who are mediums, in fact—it's just that the work they do is different than the work I was put on this earth for. For some reason, I'm well equipped to face darkness, and this is not true for all mediums. Every single one I've met just doesn't want to deal with the level of negativity I do.

I consult with mediums regularly, though. I may have a particularly difficult exorcism—especially one with a Collector or Realm Walker—and a medium will provide me psychic backup. They'll help me connect with the dead people who have passed away in a space that's possessed. Sure, I *could* talk to these recently deceased if I wanted to, but if I'm battling an entity, I usually just won't have the energy or focus. Instead, I have to be a high-tech, laser-guided missile that's zeroing in on my target: the massive entity.

Mediums will often send their clients to me. I might get a call from someone in my psychic network who'll say, "Rachel, I think there's a lot more going on in this person's life than just dealing with a loss. They're battling some hard-core darkness that only you're capable of dealing with." Thank goodness that medium knows me because, nine times out of ten, just talking to the dead was never going to help their client.

For example, a medium friend recently consulted with a woman possessed by an Ancient Trickster that was wreaking havoc on her life. Because she was aware of my work and the effect that entities can have on clients, the medium knew right away that an entity was standing in the way of her client's ability to be at peace with her long-lost mother, so she called me. When I cleared the Trickster out, not only did the woman see a clearer path to Spirit, but my medium was able to do her job.

With Spirit fully on her side, the client began to heal from the resentment and pain surrounding her mother's death.

On the flip side, I'll often recommend mediums to my clients. If a possession relates to someone who's deceased—say, the client is traumatized by her husband's death, and that led to an entity's attachment—I'll give them the number of a medium. But if a client needs closure with someone they have lost, that's not my area of expertise.

I've also helped several world-renowned mediums figure out what to do when they see entities. These people had all encountered entities while channeling and immediately stopped cold. I taught them to identify what it was they saw and how to handle the situation. But, like I said before, most mediums aren't willing to deal with the dark energy from entities. It's not that they *can't* understand what entities are—but mediums just prefer to work in the light space. I also teach them how to accept the negativity that comes from Spirit. After all, you can't appreciate the light without having seen the darkness.

The dead souls that visit during exorcisms always appear in whatever form they were at the prime of their lives. They want to be recognized, so they're often young, wrinkle-free, and good looking. Later on, I might find out that they died when they were ninety-five! Luckily, people never show up looking as they appeared at the point of death. If someone was shot, I'll never see their wounds. Maybe Spirit's being kind to me, or perhaps that's just its way of saying that the bulk of a person's life is more important than the circumstances of their death.

I had a client recently whose mother had died of breast cancer. He was guilt ridden, unable to sleep because he felt terrible that he hadn't done more to save her. He was a person already prone to depression, but he became even more vulnerable and low frequency after her death, and a Clive attached to him. He then plunged further into sadness and despair than he'd ever been in his life. His dead mother showed up—looking young and healthy—to help me with the exorcism. She reassured me that her son had done all he could during her illness and that he had nothing to feel guilty about.

I often see dead souls when I work with clients who were adopted, and they're *always* part of my client's biological family. This makes total sense when you think about it. People who are adopted often feel unwanted or unvalued. Deep down, they harbor a fear that they're worthless since they were given up at the most vulnerable time in their lives. Even if they have wonderful adoptive families, they may still feel abandoned, and entities flock to that low-frequency energy.

I also see dead people *outside* of exorcisms. Most of the time, this happens because the deceased have something incredibly important to say—and they know I'm available to hear it. Other times, these souls just want to be seen for reasons I may never understand. I suspect that something is preventing them from going back into Spirit, and they need to be heard. They'll tell me how they died, or what their life was like. I think—like my mother and the mobster I saw in the slaughterhouse—they need to come to grips with their lives before they can move on.

Sometimes, the dead have a specific message for me, which was the case with my grandmother. She and I were incredibly close while I was growing up, and she passed away when I was in my late twenties. She'd always been such a happy lady, and when she developed Alzheimer's, that didn't change. It made her sweet and simple, and—get this—she died eating ice cream. I was crushed when she passed, but deep down I knew her death was a blessing. It was her time. Death didn't feel like a huge transition because, for so many years, my grandmother had one foot on the other side.

I wasn't in a good place when my grandmother passed away. I'd just lost my house, I was lonely, and I'd had a few setbacks with my career. Losing the person I was closest to in the world was a massive emotional shock, and I got seriously depressed right away. My grandmother knew that, and she came to me two days after she passed.

My grandma was what I now call "freshly dead," and she wasn't yet ready to be seen. She hadn't learned how to compose herself in death, so she still looked sick. She was malformed, with the lower half of her body missing. People always expect that the dead are going to glow with an otherworldly beauty the moment they die, but that's not the case. It takes time for them to figure out how they're supposed to appear. My grandma hadn't had that time yet, but that didn't stop her from trying to help me. It was just like her to put me ahead of herself.

"I'm going to turn the light on for you," she said.

What does that mean? I thought. But she didn't tell me anything else. She just turned around, and I never saw her again. I know she passed back quickly into Spirit after this.

Over the next few months, I was a wreck, but then my grandmother's words sank in, and my life started to improve. I found a wonderful new place to live. My work became more fulfilling and lucrative. I began to learn things about myself and my place in the world. I put the pieces of my life back together. Just having my grandma say, "I'm not really gone. I'm here for you, you haven't been forgotten," was all I needed. It took me a while, but I found the strength and the confidence to get my life back on track.

Unsolved Mysteries

Unfortunately, not all dead people come to me with good news. In fact, sometimes they're trying to warn me about a massive, horrifying entity.

Out of respect for her family, I can't go into much detail about this, but I'm frequently visited by one of the people who died in the Cecil Hotel because of its Realm Walker. Years ago, a middle-aged woman was murdered by someone who was under the sway of this entity, yet it was attributed to a drug overdose. When I first heard about the Cecil and did some initial research, I stumbled onto a mention of the woman. I thought about her all night, then asked Spirit about her, and I think Source passed the message on. This woman's spirit was in limbo, and she knew I'd be receptive to her, so she came to me the next night.

She hung out with me for three straight days, telling the truth about her death over and over again. She still comes to me, in fact, and she only asks for one thing: that I exorcise the Cecil Hotel so the Realm Walker won't kill anyone else. When that happens, she can pass back into Source.

She's also revealed to me that, from the first day the Cecil opened its doors, murderers like Richard Ramirez, Jack Unterweger, and the person who killed her—all of whom lived in the hotel—have kept souvenirs of their killings. These include personal items like driver's licenses, jewelry, even locks of hair, and they're all still in the hotel somewhere. The murdered woman knows where they're stowed away, and she's given me very specific locations so that, one day, I can find them. They hold the key to solving both her murder and the deaths of everyone who's suffered at the hands of the Cecil's Realm Walker.

I know I'll have that chance when I exorcise the Cecil, a moment that I hope comes very soon. This woman's soul—and the spirit of everyone who died there—is hanging in the balance, unable to pass back into Spirit until the Realm Walker is gone. When it is, it may not just be the Cecil that turns around; all of downtown LA may awaken as well.

CHAPTER 14

Raising Your Frequency

The Big Picture

t's taken me years to attain the optimal mental space to do what I do. When you're battling entities every week, sometimes seven days in a row, it's hard to keep your head and your heart in a positive place. But I must. I simply can't afford to let low-frequency energy take over my life because my clients need me. And I hope I don't sound arrogant by saying this, but I think the world needs me, too.

You might be wondering how you can find for yourself the kind of hyper-psychically-aware space in which I've taught myself to exist. You may want to connect deeply with Spirit, but that takes dedication and time. What you can attain today is an increased feeling of happiness and peace. And the good news is, that's not as hard as you might think. In fact, much of what I do and how I think boils down to one thing, and it has nothing to do with mixing herb blends, speaking with the dead, or blasting entities into oblivion. The first step to forging a connection with Spirit involves raising your frequency, and there are many, many easy ways to do that.

When you raise your frequency, you know it right away. Not only will you feel excited, both physically and emotionally, but you'll sense it in your body. An increase in frequency is a shiver-down-your-spine twinge of satisfaction, as if you just scored the winning goal, had a mind-blowing orgasm, or nailed the important presentation at work. When your frequency goes up, it's like you just received the best surprise of your life. You might get the chills, sense your stomach drop, or just feel lighter. You may wonder, *Where did this feeling come from?* The truth is that it stems directly from the Higher Beings who have just come into your space. They're near you and protecting you, and they make me feel the exact same way every single time I call them into an exorcism.

This chapter provides a handful of easy-to-employ concepts that will help you raise your frequency anytime you're low. When you get yourself into a higher-frequency space, it's almost effortless to forge a full connection with Spirit—then use that connection to receive answers about tough questions you are facing in life. Eventually, you'll find yourself totally in touch with Spirit, and if you work at it, you'll be able to communicate with Higher Beings and your deceased loved ones.

I'll also outline some things that might appear to help you raise your frequency, but sometimes don't, and I'll describe the reasons why they won't. Ultimately, it's up to you as to how you choose to raise your vibration, and whether to do that work in the first place. But, my hope for you is that you won't fall into that mode of thinking. Being low frequency is unpleasant at best, and dangerous at worst.

Transactional Consciousness: Changing Your Mind-Set

Transactional consciousness is a term I use regularly, yet most people who work with the Spirit world don't seem to. You might hear mediums or psychics talking about issues related to transactional consciousness, but they'll more likely use terms like "karma," which isn't *quite* the same. The gist of transactional consciousness is this: any gesture you make that instantly puts good into the world will raise your frequency.

Both karma and transactional consciousness involve doing something good in the hopes that you'll get something even better back, but the distinction is that karma is abstract. When you put good vibes into the world just *because*, you have no idea how long it will take something positive to arrive in return. You also have no clue what that karma-inspired event could be. You could win the lottery in two days, or something entirely passive might happen to you, like narrowly missing getting shit on by a pigeon. Transactional consciousness is immediate, so it's perfect for those who think in a "these are all the things I have to get done between nine and five" kind of way. If every minute counts for you, don't just hope that karma's going to catch up with you. Try transactional consciousness. It's instant gratification.

Before I describe the many ways you can practice transactional consciousness, I want to first describe why it's so vital. Most important, when you do it, you are making a down payment on your future happiness because you're putting positivity into the world. Second, transactional consciousness is a slap in the face to entities. They want low frequency, and if you're radiating the exact opposite, entities will quickly move to another possible host.

As I've said throughout this book, people walk around in low-frequency spaces for many reasons. They experience traumatic events, they live in places or with people that make them feel awful, or they have something as simple as a bad day at work. Whatever the reason, our society accepts low frequency as one of its many norms. Getting into college is *supposed* to be stressful. It's expected that you're going to experience at least a dozen painful breakups before you meet the person of your dreams. Women go back to work after six weeks of maternity leave, full of fear and longing for their babies, because that's just how it's done. And sitting in gridlock is what you do if you need to be at work at 9 A.M. It's a bleak, sad world out there, and only the long-suffering can survive—or so we're conditioned to believe.

Worse, most of us aren't taught how to change our vibration because we don't think about life in these terms. Unless you meditate regularly, have a spiritual practice, or step outside of yourself—and into Spirit—on a regular basis, you may not even realize that your thoughts are pure energy. They have power. If you are just going about your day, nose to the grindstone, you likely feel weak, with the weight of the world on your shoulders. Your only relief might be drinking, mindless eating, zoning out to television, or sleeping. These are brain-numbing activities that distract you from the world at large, and none of them tune you into Spirit. Instead, they turn you away from it.

The first thing you need to do to combat that is realize: 1) Your feelings aren't facts. I know I sound like a therapist here, but think about this carefully. If you're hurting because of a breakup, that doesn't mean the end of the relationship is, inherently, an awful thing. You just *feel* that way. Your emotions are entirely in your mind, but they may seep into every fiber of your being, causing you to believe that everything you think defines your life. And, because you understand them as facts, you believe you can't change them. You have to trust that you're more powerful than the tide of your emotions. 2) Your true feelings, those of your highest and best self, come from your Heart Space, not the mind. The mind is often fear based, while the heart is love based. We often confuse the fear-based thoughts with true emotion because the mind is always trying to live in the past or the future, which creates anxiety and fear. The Heart Space is about feeling in the moment and living presently. If people can distinguish between the two in the moment—actively *feel* from the Heart Space—they will be able to identify this for themselves. Finally, 3) Your emotions are energy, pure and simple, and to treat them any other way is to sell yourself short. Once you start realizing that what's going on in your head is only frequency, you can begin understanding how you transfer that energy to the world around you, and everyone in it. If you're feeling low, you radiate that energy signature. It fills up all the spaces surrounding you that hold energy—which is just about everything, everywhere.

You can also cut through these many steps simply by employing transactional consciousness. That's right; even if you're experiencing something that's keeping you low frequency, you can very convincingly *not* put that negativity out there—without betraying who you are or what you've experienced. And, in doing so, you raise your own frequency, which will inevitably change your feelings and your perception.

The method is simple. All you have to do is act on something you normally wouldn't. Go against what your instincts tell you to do and put forth a gesture that's beneficial to another person. For example, buy food for the homeless person you normally pass by, thinking that any help you give will only enable them. Act against your impulses and make the decision that feeding that person, in that moment, will assist them.

If you have a coworker you've never connected with, offer to bring her coffee one morning. If you see trash on the sidewalk, pick it up. Or if the person in front of you in the Chipotle line is holding everyone up because she can't find fifty cents, just put down a dollar and tell her to keep the change. You don't have to change the world. Just make one tiny gesture of kindness that is different from your normal pattern, and sit back and watch the good energy start flowing.

What you're doing may not *seem* selfish, but it is. In a good way! Selfishness isn't always a bad thing, especially if it helps someone else at the same time. Raising your frequency makes you radiate a good energy that then changes the frequency of everyone around you *and* the space in which you move.

In fact, I've found that inherently selfish or narcissistic people absolutely love transactional consciousness because it makes them feel so good, so quickly. You might think that crowd is limited to my celebrity clients, but it's not. When a person—whoever they might be—employs transactional consciousness for a quick feel-good boost, it begins a pattern of behavior that they want to continue. Suddenly, all the wealth and power in the world feels meaningless as they discover the power of good deeds.

Meditation

I heard you groan when you read that word. Remember? I can sense things about you, and I could just *feel* what you were thinking: *Ugh, meditation. You expect me to sit in silence for five minutes and think about nothing? For the love of God, I'm a busy person!*

Trust me, I understand why you dislike meditation, and for many of my clients, it's impossible for me to convince them to try it. Some people love meditation, while others can't make their brains shut up. If meditation is your thing—or you think there's a chance that it might be—I highly recommend the practice because I know it will raise your frequency. Just taking five minutes where you can shut out the barrage of thoughts in your brain and listen to the sound of your breath will calm you down, give you peace, and send good energy flowing through your mind and body that will certainly raise your frequency.

If you don't feel comfortable trying meditation on your own, there are apps that might help you. Breathe, available on iTunes, is one of my favorites. It allows you to check boxes on how you feel that day (Happy? Nervous? Excited?), then offers several guided meditations of varying lengths based on how you're feeling. Just plug in your earbuds, find a comfortable spot on the couch, and open the app.

You can also record your own voice based on any number of meditations on the Internet or in books, or you can google "meditation scripts" and find thousands online.

Meditation in Song

Like I said, I usually don't push strict meditation on clients after they walk out of my Spirit Room. Instead, more often than not, I'll recommend singing. That's right, just singing a little song. Turn on some music you love and sing along. Or, go a cappella. You don't have to have any actual talent. This is all about the practice.

Singing raises your vibration immediately, and it feels good because it's an instant boost of positive energy. If you think about it, children start singing not long after they learn to talk, and they do it happily in their beds at night, in circle time at school, or while playing "Ring Around the Rosie" with their friends. Children are the purest, most connected-to-Source beings on the planet, so it is no coincidence that they inherently know how to soothe themselves—and feel joy—through song. It's their direct link to Higher Beings, who flood in when they raise their frequency.

I always sing before exorcisms. Once I've set everything up and feel fully prepared, I'll put on songs I like and sing along with them till my client shows up. Just warming up my vocal cords energizes me and raises my frequency. When my energy is high, my connection to Spirit and Higher Beings is cleaner, which makes it easier for them to work with me and vice versa.

Some people assume I might chant during exorcisms, or just to commune with Spirit. I don't, and that's because it doesn't really appeal to me. I also think that chanting, OM-ing, and opening up your chakras isn't all that relatable to most people, so I want to teach my clients (and anyone reading this book) that there are so many other ways to become conscious.

You don't have to chant. You don't have to pray. Just sing your heart out whenever you're feeling bad. I promise it'll help raise your frequency.

Mindful Connection

For a lot of people, meditation to clear the mind just isn't feasible. After all, your mind's been running the show for most of your life. So I often recommend that clients try to forge a deeper connection with Spirit in another way: by opening their hearts.

I call this "Mindful Connection," and it's easy. All you have to do is sit quietly wherever you can, for however long you feel you can. And in that space and time, ask aloud to connect with Spirit. At that point, you will receive information—thoughts, ideas, visuals, or words. Just trust that. Don't swat those ideas away as nothing.

Do this once a day for thirty days. In the beginning, depending on how blocked up or low frequency you are, you might feel like you're not receiving anything. But if you do it for the full thirty days, the connection *will* gradually open.

Gratitude

It sounds so simple that it's almost ridiculous, but just waking up every day and forcing yourself to remember what you're grateful for will do wonders for your frequency. You can't only *realize* the things you're happy about, though. You also need to verbalize them, making a point to acknowledge each and every one in a very deliberate fashion.

I understand that expressing gratitude can be more difficult than it sounds. A lot of people have *really* tough lives, and the thought of feeling grateful about anything is laughable. And even if you're generally happy most of the time, being thankful every. single. damn. morning can be tough. I'm no exception. I have a beautiful life. I make my living doing things I love. I have the opportunity to be around amazing people, and most days I feel like Goth Supergirl battling the dark forces of the universe. Yet I still wake up and feel crappy sometimes. There are many, many days when even minor things affect me.

This is just part of being human. For all of us—even the most high-frequency individuals like myself—there are some days when everything piles up, and you're like, *Forget it.*

Yet I still force myself to verbalize my gratitude, even if it's only for the pillow I'm about to lie back down on and the snooze button I'm about to hit.

I try not to speak about gratitude in an overly metaphysical, woo-woo way because that alienates a lot of people. Most average Americans are run-down working for a living, raising kids, rushing around, stressed out, and they surely resent some New Age chick who rolls out of bed at 7 A.M., fresh as a daisy, and says, "Life is great!" I get it. Being thankful for anything when you're depressed, in pain, broke, or your kid is screaming is hard, but, trust me, force yourself. Take ten seconds and verbalize something, anything, that makes you happy. It could be something as simple as the soft toilet paper you just bought on sale or the fact that your car's coming out of the shop that day. I promise you, if you just say *something*, you'll feel your frequency go up.

Manifesting

This recommendation isn't ripped straight from *The Secret*, I promise. I do have tremendous respect for the book's philosophy, which centers on the law of attraction, and I believe, just like the book teaches, that you can manifest the things you want in life simply by verbalizing them. I also believe that if you stop going on and on about what's negative in your life, you will stop bringing all the unpleasant, unhappy stuff in.

But my version of manifesting isn't about telling yourself—again and again and again—that you're going to get a new car, and, then, *voila*! There it is. Manifesting is more than just thinking positively or willing something to happen. It's about stopping the misery train before it reaches the station—that is, refusing to think in an unconstructive, negative fashion.

For example, let's say you didn't get the raise you were really counting on. It would be so easy to go home, make yourself a stiff drink, and start complaining to your husband. You could say, "Since I won't be getting that bigger paycheck, we won't be able to afford a down payment on a house. This is terrible!" That kind of thinking won't get you anywhere, and it just increases your negative feelings. Then, you might go into your kitchen and fix yourself another drink. Or three.

Instead, you need to flip the script. Say out loud: "This didn't happen at the time I wanted it to, but there has to be a reason for that. Maybe that house wasn't right for me. I just have to focus on something else now." Sooner or later, I promise you, you'll get the house that's best for you. It may take time, but the right one will come along in due course.

You can shift your thinking by verbalizing the positive. And when you stop, collect yourself for a moment, and try to see—perhaps glimmering in the far-off distance—something that might one day make you happy, you'll actually feel a twinge of something positive. Congratulations! You've just raised your frequency.

The sad fact is that most people only verbalize what's wrong in their lives. Negative things just happen, for no apparent reason. But if you tell yourself, "I'm amazing. I'm incredible. The universe loves me, and if something didn't come to pass, it's because it just wasn't my time," you'll actually feel better because it's the truth.

I do this every single day, and it's now become second nature to me. I don't even have to force it. Instead, it's become a natural way of speaking about how the events of my life have unfolded.

This isn't to say I don't grieve. You have to allow yourself to mourn when truly bad things happen because it's unnatural not to feel pain. Grief is a healthy part of the process of acceptance and healing, and I'd never shame you for it. But when you shift your thinking and verbalize the positive rather than the negative, your period of grieving becomes shorter. Even when I feel destroyed by something, I now only mourn for a few hours. I experience intense sadness, then pick myself up and return to my normal awareness.

Clearing the Collective

I do find it harder to be high-minded and high frequency when bad things happen out in the world. For years, I've struggled with how to process natural disasters, upsetting political developments, terrorism, or the plight of people and animals around the world. I've never been a news junkie, and I think that's because my feelings are so deep that seeing the awful things in the world at large hits me too hard.

Yet I've come to learn that I have to be prepared in order to face these events.

The way I've done this is by utilizing a process called "clearing the collective." This is a method of thinking advocated by many world-famous healers, and it involves blessing any kind of negative event that comes to pass. The blessing isn't the spiritual equivalent of a shrug-off; it's a way to shift negative energy so that it pools together. In essence, the collective feels the pain.

The second aspect of clearing the collective involves you acknowledging the good actions you've taken to better the world, and using them to counter the negative events around you. This is exactly what I do whenever I speak to one of my good friends, Marc Ching, who runs a charity called the Animal Hope and Wellness Foundation.

I'm the world's biggest animal lover, but I struggle with what Marc does for a living. He and members of his organization go to places like Yulin, China, where dogs are killed in slaughterhouses for human consumption. Because some people believe that if an animal suffers, its meat will taste better, many of these dogs aren't killed in humane ways. There is also evidence that some of them are, in fact, stolen house pets. Marc is such an angel on earth that he walks right into these slaughterhouses and snatches the dogs from death's door. Workers at these horrible places have put machetes to his head and threatened to kill him, so every time Marc leaves on a business trip, he tells his family, "I might not come back, so just know I love you."

I champion absolutely everything Marc does, and I've donated to his group. But I can hardly think about those poor dogs, let alone talk to him about them. I can't stomach looking at the photos he emails from his trips, and I really struggle listening to his stories. I love animals just a little too much, and it breaks my heart to think of them in pain.

I've accepted that I'm just not strong enough to process that kind of suffering, and that's okay. You might be like me. You may struggle to read the daily news, or you might be paralyzed by a terrible loss within your family. Take relief in the fact that it's not your responsibility to feel the weight of the world on your shoulders, and you're not doomed to be low frequency for eternity! Plus, Spirit won't judge you. Grief and sadness are perfectly acceptable, and we can't all process things the same way. As long as we do our part by adding to the collective, you can raise your frequency *and* make the world a better place.

I add to the collective by destroying entities. After I do my part, other people do the dirty work that I can't, like rescuing dogs from slaughterhouses. Say you're a paramedic. You probably think: *I'm strong because I can go into places where people are hurt or dying, and I help make them okay. That's my job.* Yet, you might break down when you find out you mother has cancer. Your frequency level might take a temporary hit, but you're likely still high energy because you've done your part for the collective. That's your gift to the world.

Communing with the Spirit World

Each and every one of you has the ability to be fully connected to Spirit. Not just that, but every person on this planet has the ability to speak to those who have passed. Both of these skills are part and parcel of the same thing: they're inherent gifts we have within us, granted by Spirit, who desperately desires a closeness with us. Unfortunately, most people don't use these abilities because they either don't believe they exist or don't know how to tap into them. If they did the world would be a much happier and healthier place for everyone.

Ready to try? Let me teach you how.

First, you have to trust yourself. You cannot second-guess your connection to Spirit in any way. That connection is what makes communing with the Spirit world possible.

Second, you need to realize that Spirit speaks to you in whatever manner suits you best. For example, I talked about automatic writing earlier. That's one of the easiest ways for me to connect to Spirit, and I think it's because I'm open to it. I'm a word person, so I like to see scribbles on the page. Some people are spiritually drawn to sounds, so listening to or making music will forge a connection to Spirit. It opens their soul and moves them, making them happy and raising their frequency. Others are more attuned to visuals and symbols, so Spirit will communicate with them through images. Spirit may send them flashes of things that they pass off as coincidence—like repeating numbers moving through their minds or people around them saying the same phrases again and again. There is no such thing as coincidence; it's simply Spirit creating synchronicity. It's Source's first and foremost way to grab your attention.

Everyone has a method through which Spirit can reach them, but many people don't trust the messages. They'll hear or see a sign—like the aforementioned repeated numbers, feathers falling from the sky, coins scattered on the ground, or their deceased parents' voices passing through their minds, all undeniably from Spirit—and chalk them up to instinct or coincidence. I want to run up and grab them and say, "No, it's not! It's Spirit!"

Mediums will tell you the exact same thing. When I've asked medium friends how they speak to the dead, their answer is always simply "I just let it in." You must trust the connection. If you ask a question of Spirit, you will get an answer. That's how Source works, and that's what you need to look for—in whatever form is meant for you.

You might not actually *see* a dead relative, get an answer to a burning question, or receive step-by-step instructions, but Spirit will reveal the person or the answer to you nonetheless. The minute you get a sign, you have to go with it, even if on the surface it makes no sense at all.

For example, once during an exorcism I was so connected to Spirit that I got a visual of a jar of honey. For a split second I was tempted to ask, "Why the hell would a jar of honey pop into my head?" But I verbalized what I'd seen, and my client responded accordingly. "Oh, yes, honey! My grandfather used to keep bees." Her grandfather was trying to communicate with her through me. Spirit sent a signal—a visual of honey—to represent that.

Some people are just born less connected than others, so learning to commune with Spirit and tap into an extrasensory ability might prove to be more of a challenge. Such was the case with a recent client.

As I said, I've never met anyone else who fully acknowledges that they can see entities. I've always suspected that someone else like me is out there, but so far I haven't shaken hands with them. Recently, however, a famous young actor—whom I'll call Mr. Celebrity—came to my Spirit Room for an exorcism, and I was blown away by how similar his energy signature was to mine.

"I've been able to manipulate my own energy since I was a kid," he said.

Oh my God, so have I! I thought.

"And I think sometimes I see and feel things, but I'm not sure."

Like . . . ?

"But then I got famous so young, so fast, that I put it out of my mind. I thought doing drugs would suppress it, but they only make me sense things more." He paused. "What do you think is happening to me? Is there something else out there?"

I wanted to jump up, grab him by the shoulders, and beg him to tell me he could see entities just like me. But that's not my place. Like any person grappling with their connection to Spirit, he needed to discover it himself—if indeed he has that ability at all.

Mr. Celebrity had a few garden-variety Clives that I was able to remove without any problem, and he left my Spirit Room saying he felt much better. Then a few days later, he called me.

"Rachel," he said, "I need to tell you that I've been sensing certain energies and a lot more since my exorcism. Like I did when I took drugs, but more clearly. These feelings, these images, make sense to me. I don't want to block them out."

"That's good," I responded. "Let's reconnect because I want to show you how to harness that."

I haven't seen Mr. Celebrity again, but I hope I will. I think that, like me, he has a gift that he can use for good, but he has to dedicate himself to the work. He needs to acknowledge his gift, embrace it, and use Spirit to comprehend it.

I'm sure I can be of assistance. If he came back to see me, I'd open him up to his gift by helping him master the fundamentals. First, I'd teach him about recognizing frequency. I'd use the energy trick I mentioned earlier in the book, where you hold a rock in your hand, then feel its frequency shift. Then I'd teach him about earth energy by taking him to a place where something awful happened; a spot that was particularly low frequency. There, I'd guide him through how to sense the earth's vibration. These exercises sound so simplistic, but they ease a person into connecting with Spirit, which is a gradual process. It's like a weak muscle that you have to exercise to make stronger. But when you practice, you open yourself up and start listening to Spirit, and then everything changes.

◎

Just like me, many of my clients have had issues with their mothers. Often, these buried feelings bubble to the surface during their exorcisms. Even if someone loves their mom dearly, and even if she's still alive, she may haunt them—literally or metaphorically. My client Daniel Knauf, a television writer and producer, didn't receive a visitation from his deceased mother's spirit during his exorcism, but he did get symbols and visions about her. His experience isn't just fascinating; it's also the perfect example of how sometimes Spirit sends messages in the most remarkable ways.

DAN

I consider myself an existentialist and experientialist. I really try to experience as many things as possible because it feeds my storytelling. I met Rachel through a mutual friend, and because I'd never before met an exorcist, I thought, *This should be interesting.* We got together to drink a bottle of wine, sat and chatted, and got to know each other. Then, I decided, *You know what? Experientialist that I am, I think I'll go through an exorcism. Let's see what this is like.* So I set up an appointment with Rachel for the following month.

Rachel took me into a little room in the back of her house and started the process. She didn't make any incantations or anything; she just called on various saints and angels. I was lying on a bed with my eyes closed. Then, I started having very lucid hallucinations. At first, I saw a big, full moon, and immediately the feeling that came to mind was about my mother. I began to see what looked like a piece of rotting wood or log that was on the ground in the forest. It was infested with black pill bugs. I could hear them talking to each other in a sort of chattering sound. It was a kind of communication. Then all of a sudden, I witnessed what appeared to be an antigravity ray, and the bugs were pulled up and out of this log. The sensation I had was like stitches being removed—like someone was pulling thread out of my chest. It was all very vivid, and I kept thinking, *These are things that are in me, and they have something to do with my mom.*

I was in a chaotic place in my life. I'd had a marriage collapse after 32 years. I hadn't been single since I was 21 years old, yet, all of a sudden, I'd been thrust into the dating world. I was also dealing with the fact that both my parents had died three and five years before that. Suddenly, I was an orphan, and I was adrift. I had trouble interpreting why I felt that way, and why it was so tied to Mom.

Since my exorcism, I've turned my thoughts to my mother. Something told me, "You've got to think about your mom a little bit," and so I realized my mother's role in who I was attracted to. My father had left my mom when I was twelve and I'd been thrown into being the man of the house. I wasn't psychologically prepared for that. Later, I got into a pattern of finding women who I rescued. I was responsible for them—just like I'd been with Mom.

My exorcism helped settle me. It made me focus on getting involved with people who weren't black holes of crazy need. The women I've since gotten involved with have even helped that process along.

CHAPTER 15

Home Ex-Onomics

N ow that I've explored some psychological and emotional strategies that help raise frequency and get you closer to Spirit, let's turn to some easy, at-home approaches. Entities are especially active in our homes—our sanctuaries, where we spend our most private moments—so please take to heart how important it is to fight them there. Luckily, doing so is not difficult. The simple things I describe in this chapter may alter your energy just enough to prevent a dangerous attachment.

Herbs, Minerals, and Resins
That Keep the Entities at Bay

Plants, minerals, and resins are well known to have many powerful healing qualities. This is also true when it comes to raising your frequency. Burning them can easily increase the good energy in your environment. They smell good, they change the atmosphere of the room, and entities hate them. You may have heard about the "cleansing" properties of burning sage, but there are many herbs that go far beyond sage.

When a client comes in for an exorcism, I read their energy and tailor my recipes accordingly. Perfecting my blends has been a process; I've learned how to do it through trial and error and communing with Spirit. Since most of my exorcisms are, thankfully, for low-level entities like Clives, I blend herbs and resins that I'm comfortable recommending for you to use at home. Sometimes, however, herbs like these just aren't strong enough to battle a particularly malicious entity like a Trickster. I need to blend something so powerful that, when I burn it, it's like an atom bomb going off in the room. These include:

Wolfsbane: A purple, poisonous flowering plant that's frequently used in traditional Chinese medicine and Ayurvedic healing practices. It usually comes as a dried root and is available online or in apothecary shops. Be careful, though! It's *highly* poisonous.

Hemlock: This is the lacy, triangular plant that's famous for killing Socrates. He drank it in a potion, but I burn a powder that's made of the plant's dried leaves and berries.

The odor is musty, and while some people find it a little off-putting, I love it.

Blue lotus: This is a gorgeous water lily that has a sedative effect that's so powerful it's considered a class 1 drug in some countries. Like hemlock, it's available in liquid form, but you can buy it as a powder, or as a chunky mixture of crushed flowers.

I love all of these plants; not only do they smell absolutely divine when you're burning them (especially blue lotus, which is used in a lot of perfumes), but they create a fantastic aura in the room that relaxes my clients and scares their entities.

Unfortunately, all of them are highly poisonous, so I use them only when necessary. Some people believe that these drugs cause hallucinations, but that's not actually true. They just should not be employed unless the situation really warrants it—and even then I let my clients be the final judge of whether they are comfortable. I've spent *years* researching their properties, I'm meticulous about using them in small, precise amounts, and I always properly ventilate my Spirit Room. Using them in your home without proper training isn't advised. If you go too far with them, you risk poisoning yourself, which may involve a lot of incredibly unpleasant side effects like nausea, vomiting, disorientation, or worse.

Some of my favorite, nontoxic minerals, plants, and resins—all of which you can burn at home—are easy to find online or in metaphysical stores. I can't promise that burning them will actually rid your body of entities—the demons are usually too deeply rooted to the darkness or trauma inside you—but doing so will certainly prevent others from coming in, and can also help raise your frequency.

Frankincense: The Christian church frequently uses this in exorcisms. I love it because it raises the frequency of the room, quickly. Not everyone loves the smell— it's a little heavy and very masculine—but everyone responds to it. You typically find frankincense as an essential oil, which can be burned, but I like to use the dry resin.

Copal: This is a tree resin from the copal tree. The Mayans and the indigenous people of Mexico and Central America used this throughout their history as an incense, and it can often be found in religious or communal ceremonies. When it burns, copal smells very clean, and that's exactly what it does. It is *excellent* at clearing the air, and entities are absolutely repelled by it. I prefer copal resin sticks, which a lot of Spanish bodegas carry. You can also buy loose copal resin, which are little stones that look similar to amber. Copal comes in black and white, and it honestly doesn't matter which color you use. Burn it several times a day throughout your house, in whatever form you prefer. You can also choose to burn it at night, when entities like Tricksters or the Sandman may be circulating.

Sulfur (**ALSO CALLED** *Brimstone*): Before you rush out and buy this, just know that sulfur does *not* smell good. A lot of people have sensitivities to sulfur, in fact— it makes them feel nauseated, or even vomit—so I'm always careful to ask a client if this is a problem before an exorcism. Sulfur's a mineral, so you can crush it, or I buy incense discs (made of charcoal) and light the sulfur

Sulfur (if not sulfur sensitive): This is a banishing agent for entities

Mullein: For protection against an entity that might be hovering in a space, but not attached at the time

Elderflower: For prosperity and instant health. It's high vibrational and brings about joy

Solomon's seal: For protection against hovering entities as well as low vibrational deceased people

Angelica root: For protection from entities. Also increases the effectiveness of the other herbs used

Juniper berries: For protection from accidents and physical harm associated with entities

RAISING THE VIBRATION OF A SPACE

Use this blend when something feels "off" in a space like your office or home. If there's an energy you don't recognize, a smell you don't like, or if something in the air just doesn't feel good, this is what you want to burn. This blend can effectively transmute the negative energy of a person who was in the space as well (a coworker, an ex, etc.), and can diminish old negative energies (imprints of deaths, fights, abuse, etc.).

Sage: For protection and clearing

Copal: For protection, increasing positive vibration, and cleansing

Frankincense: Purifies the atmosphere and increases emotional/physical health

Rose petals: These bring love energy into the space

Damask rose: Has a very powerful uplifting energy, associated with archangels

Cassia: Stimulates your own psychic abilities and creates energetic barriers

Lemon balm: For communion with goddess energy, this adds personal energy

Orange peel: To create joy energy

Dragon's blood: This enhances and amplifies all of the above

MANIFESTING ABUNDANCE

This is a great blend to burn when your frequency feels high, and you're ready to bring something positive into your life. Use it while meditating or to help intensify your focus on what you want to manifest. This blend will aid you in attracting what you desire while helping you gently release what no longer vibrates at your frequency.

Alkanet: Attracts money, luck, and abundance quickly

Cinnamon: Attracts energy, love, strength, and inspiration

Cumin: Cleanses and attracts love and passion

Corn silk: Assists and works with the law of attraction

Oregano: Helps with health, love, and potency

Oakmoss: Attracts money

Cedar chips: Attracts money

Cinquefoil: For prophecy and dreams

Nutmeg: Attracts money

Star anise: For luck and clairvoyance

Catnip: Attracts pet magic, beauty, love, and happiness

HOW TO USE HERBS IN MEDITATION

I recommend using copal as you meditate; the combination of meditation and burning copal raises your frequency and protects you from other people's negative energy. To do this, take one stick of copal resin, place it on a table next to you, and light it. Wait till it's burning sufficiently, then seat yourself somewhere comfortable close enough to smell it. The scent doesn't have to be overpowering, just enough that you can sense it as you inhale it from afar.

Sit quietly in a spot you find comfortable, without distractions. Close your eyes and visualize yourself filled with fire, the flames licking your toes, extending up your legs, and filling your core. Imagine yourself letting go of whatever balled-up knot you may feel in your stomach. Imagine the flames are burning away your pain, unleashing the entities that inhabit you.

Next, watch the flames move up your body, and breathe in the scent of the copal. Allow the fire and the scent to warm you from the inside out. Let them travel throughout your body for as long or as little as you like—even for only five minutes. Doing this for even a small amount of time each day will help raise your vibration, keeping negative energy and low-level entities far away from you.

Candles, Stones, and Crystals

I love candles, and I have filled both my house and my Spirit Room with them. Whenever I see a candle that I like, I snatch it up, take it home, and inscribe it with whatever statement or mantra appeals to me at that moment. If I have a little more time and a particular purpose in mind, I might melt part of a candle and infuse it with my own herb blends. You don't have to buy a certain kind of candle to raise your frequency; just purchase whatever makes you feel good.

I also always have stones around my house. I do this primarily because, after an exorcism, my clients are flooded with high-frequency energy, and a stone placed in their hand will absorb it from their body. Because every person is different, I don't always use the same stone, and sometimes I'll go through two or three till I find one that my client is comfortable with.

Why is excess energy a bad thing, you ask? Because the body just isn't capable of keeping it for long periods. Imagine you wake up one day and decide to run a marathon—yet you've never before run a mile. If you lace up your shoes and hit the road, your body will be shocked and wear down quickly. It would be too much for you. The same holds true if you store too much energy.

Holding a stone in the palm of your hand relaxes you. It's mindfulness at its most basic, and I recommend finding a comfortable spot to sit in, then centering yourself with a stone in your hand. Like I said, it'll pull out any excess energy—positive or negative—that you have flowing through you.

There are more classes of stone than I can name, but most people prefer the mineral variety, like rose quartz or pyrite. Others like gemstones such as amethyst, quartz, or jade. But, if a piece of gravel from your driveway appeals to you, go ahead and keep that by your bedside. I'm no one to judge.

I also recommend putting crystals, especially those that are standing point (obelisks—the ones that are shaped like the Washington Monument) in the corners of your home. You should face the crystals toward each other, on their sides so that the points are turned inward. You can also stand them straight up, though in my personal experience, facing them toward each other does a better job clearing the energy in your space. This is because energy is focused in the points, and when they face each other, you create an energetically cleared space within. This is called gridding. Some people are drawn to geodes, but it really comes down to personal taste.

You can also put crystals in the corners of every room in your house, or just in the rooms you use the most. It doesn't matter what kind of crystal you choose, but whatever it is, it should resonate with you. There are a million different varieties of quartz, obsidian, amethyst, apatite, jasper, citrine, in as many different colors. Just go for the ones you feel drawn to.

The thing to bear in mind is that you should always wash your crystals at least once a week, because they tend to absorb a lot of bad, negative energy. I put mine in a Himalayan saltwater bath, or I place them outside in the sun during the day or overnight under the moon to keep them fresh. I know this sounds like some kind of pagan witch ritual—and, actually, it is—but it's what I do.

High Frequency at Home

I have no mandate about how you should organize or arrange your home to raise the frequency inside. Creating a high-energy space that will repel entities is about putting together something that makes you happy. Hoarding of anything like cats, clothes, or cans of food probably won't make your heart sing—and it most likely signals an underlying problem—so I do recommend that you maintain a clean home.

Personally, I love living by graveyards. They're peaceful, full of light, well manicured, full of meaning, and beautiful to me. If I found the house of my dreams, and it was facing a cemetery, I'd cash out my savings and put down a deposit immediately. But that's just me. You might find that a window facing a bunch of tombstones isn't great for your mood.

I will say this: if you have numerous antiques, collectibles, paintings, and other things that have been passed down through many hands over many years, take the time to clean them. If you purchase these items, make sure you cleanse them with copal before you bring them home, as you have no idea of the space from which they came. That amazing oil painting you bought at an estate sale in Pasadena? The last guy who owned it could have had a Collector in his house. Even if these old objects don't carry an entity, they'll definitely have a vibrational element about them. That's just the nature of things with a lot of history; they've picked up the energy of the various hands they've passed through, and you need to make them yours, 100 percent entity-free.

I've found that most people are happier if they have a room of their own to work. It's only logical; if you have a place where you can regroup, gather your thoughts, and have an uninterrupted mental space where you can commune with Spirit, you'll likely be a cheerier person. Like I said before, I can't live in a place that doesn't have room for me to do my Spirit work. Not just for my clients, but for myself. I also have my blue, egg-shaped chair, and it makes me happy each and every time I see it. It's a sacred space just for me, so big I can sit inside it and feel sublimely at peace. I recommend the same for you.

The one thing that you *must*, without hesitation, get out of your house so you can raise your frequency are people who cause you problems. Spouses or roommates who drive you crazy, older children who have overstayed their welcome (and are perfectly capable of living on their own), or a really sloppy, irritating, overly dependent partner is an individual who is lowering your energy. No candle or geode is going to fix this. Even if you come to see me for an exorcism, nothing will change if you simply return to your bad relationships.

Obviously, sometimes we don't have choices and end up in spaces—or with people—that we don't like or don't want around. You might be getting a divorce and need to stay in the same home for complex reasons having to do with money or children. Those kinds of issues may be inevitable. Just do everything you can to keep your frequency high, on your own, using the techniques I've taught you.

Food

You are what you eat, as the saying goes, and the same is true when it comes to the Spirit world. That's why I am a vegetarian, and have been for five years. I didn't become one sooner only because I wasn't spiritually aware. I grew up a meat eater, and switching over was part of a process of upgrading my life. I'm not making a political statement, or demanding that you make this same choice for yourself. I just want you to know the facts about what you put in your mouth.

The truth is that food alters your frequency. If you live off Cheetos and other junk *all* the time, you're probably not going to feel your best, and that lowers your frequency, too. If you typically eat healthy food with a higher purpose in mind, your body and energy will thank you. Just know that it's fine to eat pasta and ice cream. You don't have to follow a raw food diet or exist on green juice. That's unreasonable, and a connection to Spirit is not all about what's on your plate. You don't have to purify everything in your life to become more conscious.

There are, however, certain "grounding" foods that help put Spirit back in the body. Think about how you feel when you're sitting around the Thanksgiving dinner table, full of salty foods like mashed potatoes and gravy with a nice coating of red wine. You feel full and settled. You're not fidgety and nervous; you want to rest or sleep. Meat, salt, and alcohol are grounding foods, and when you're spiritually off or a little spacey, they can help settle you. Since I don't eat meat, after an exorcism I'll stuff myself with other fatty things, like pizza, pasta, or cake. The fattier, the better, and they certainly don't have to be pure or 100 percent healthy. Sure, I think a clean diet is something you should aim for, but occasional pizza or cake is fine.

However, if you're trying to cleanse, I recommend staying away from foods that will make you want to crawl into a ball and take a nap. It's just common sense; eat vegetables, grains, and fresh fruit, which will get you buzzing and keep that energy up. And if you can manage to eat vegetarian or vegan, definitely do it. You'll be consuming pure high frequency, with absolutely no pain involved.

CHAPTER 16

Now That You Know . . .

Because I've got my head in the Spirit world half the time, you might assume that I can predict the future, even a little. I have a second sense about a lot of things, but I can't tell you what the next day—much less the next few years— might hold.

That said, I do have a sense of what kinds of spiritual forces will affect us in the future—and what you can do about them.

To be frank, 2016 was a batshit crazy year for everyone. Whether you're white, black, Republican, or Democrat, it didn't matter. The weirdness of 2016 has nothing to do with politics, the environment, or the zillion celebrities who passed into the pop culture Spirit world. All of these events were just symptoms of the fact that 2016 was the real 2012.

Huh? Let me clarify.

Perhaps you recall how December 12, 2012, was supposed to be a monumental moment astronomically, culturally, environmentally, and socially. The New Age community thought that date marked the beginning of a period of massive transformation, while the Mayan calendar predicted that, on 12/12/12, the world was going to end. Yet, not much happened. The clock kept ticking, 2012 retired into 2013, and life continued. According to polls, only 6 percent of people were anxious about the end of 2012, but just like Y2K, the hype was just that . . . hype.

Instead, all the bottled-up social, political, and cultural angst that was predicted to explode in 2012 came to a head in 2016 and has continued into 2017. *So* much change has happened: the United States' political system was upended, fake news and social media became the real news, and it was the hottest year on record (after the previous two hottest years on record). You might assume this chaos—and what a lot of people consider a doomsday scenario—is happening because of our political leaders, the media, and overindustrialization. But the truth is that millions of people across the world are suddenly being activated and becoming more conscious than they've ever been. They're realizing that their energy—and how they use it—affects everyone and everything around them. I'm so connected to Spirit that I can feel this shift—I sense the energy—but we can all see on social media and in the news that people are becoming more aware of others, of how we live, of our resources, of animals, and more. Almost a million people around the world marched through the streets on one single day calling for activism and change. That wasn't just about politics; people have woken up, and our collective consciousness has come to a head.

The Mayans were wrong about 2012. The apocalypse didn't happen. The only thing that died was an ailing, aging belief system. 2016 signaled a new flood of consciousness, and anyone who opens their eyes and ears can learn something from it.

You *have* to do this. People who remain committed to doing the same things they've always done will stay in a state of unconsciousness. We're at a point in society where we are being forced to wake up, and if we don't, I believe the consequences will be dire. But if we do, there's a chance for us to become better as human beings and treat the world better.

Get out of your bubble. You can't remain in the dark. I'm not saying you have to live your life exactly like I live mine, but don't do anything with blinders on. For example, if you eat meat, be aware of your environmental impact, how the meat industry operates, and just what the animals you're consuming experience before they end up on your plate. If you get your news only from one news source—and think it's the word of God—you should change that. Read lots and lots of papers and watch many different news shows so you can be *truly* informed before you tweet about what's going on in the world. Your actions have consequences, and a truly conscious person understands what they are.

I know I sound like a crazy person, but there are many underground groups out there, and they're affecting everything we do. These can be power players in Hollywood, small groups of influential politicians, or bankers who decide which way the financial tide is shifting on any given day. I receive calls from members of secret, influential organizations all the time, and in 2016, it happened more than ever. The collective unconscious broke open, and a huge number of powerful people came forward to me saying, "I need to get out of this group. It's time for me to change my life." They wanted to raise their frequencies and add to the collective, and that altered the energy of the entire world.

I—and a lot of spiritualists I am exposed to—can sense that this phenomenon is going to continue through 2020. So now is the time to share this information with as many people as possible.

This is why my calling as an exorcist is more important than ever. I work with individuals who have audiences of *millions*. If I can help a person on the global stage be healthier spiritually, that person has the potential to make positive change with all of their fans and followers. It doesn't matter if they're politicians, directors, actors, or musicians; every time they open their mouths to voice an opinion, or tweet about their vision for the world, their fans listen to them. I think it's their moral duty to try to raise the consciousness of those who follow them. They need to speak the truth, push a positive agenda, and put good out there in the world. There are too many poisonous lies, too much nasty rhetoric and flat-out meanness going on online and out in the world today. If someone famous can be a good example, they may exert a positive influence in their little corner of the universe. And that's a good thing.

Even if you're not a real influencer, there are still things you can do. The first is to try to keep your frequency as high as possible. You don't have to spend every second trying to be high-minded. Just do one random act of kindness in the name of transactional consciousness every day, and that will keep your good energy buzzing.

The other thing you can and should do is question everything. Don't take anyone's word (not even mine!) as the word of

God. Ask yourself profound questions, like, "Am I living my life the best way possible?" and simple questions like, "Should I buy organic fruit or conventional fruit?" Almost every decision you make has repercussions, so pausing before you act—and thinking about possible outcomes—can send ripples through the collective in incredibly powerful ways.

Believe me, Spirit will give you the right answer if you just stop for a minute and ask. If you have a decision—big or small—to make, hold the options in your head for a minute, say to yourself, "Which one should I choose?" and then trust. You'll feel the answer deep in your bones. That's a message from Spirit. You may think your brain is the one doing all the work, but the truth is that if you ask, you'll feel the answer inside you. As you begin to listen closely, you'll know you have the solution when everything else seems illogical. In fact, everything else *is* illogical and just plain wrong. End of story.

Spirit is simple, and it always has the answer. Humans—our egos, traumas, and the entities that flock to us because of them— are the ones who make things complicated.

From now to 2020, it's going to be more important than ever to remember that. The world is at a pivotal point, in flux between dark energy and light energy, but we have the ability to choose high frequency if we only put our minds to it and trust. Try as hard as you can to know where and what your strengths are, focus on them, and believe in Spirit. It will always—always—lead you the right way.

That, of course, is in the opposite direction from entities.

I hope this book has shown you that, if you awaken your heart and try to forge a relationship with Spirit, you won't just change your life—you can help alter the fabric of the universe as well. If you learn to connect and truly *feel* things, everything else will open up. As a society, we're so unconscious, and we've spent far too much time not questioning the belief systems we've had for decades. Now is the time to change that. I hope I've helped show you how.

ACKNOWLEDGMENTS

A huge thank-you goes out to Yfat Reiss Gendell, Danny Sherman, and Josh Kesselman for their tireless efforts in bringing this book to fruition. Thank you, Sarah Durand, for working through so much information—a lifetime's worth!—and figuring out how all the puzzle pieces fit together. That was no easy task, and you did an amazing job. Thank you, Carrie Thornton, for being so thorough and believing so very strongly in this story. Thank you for feeling that this was a message that people needed to receive.

From Foundry, special thanks to Jessica Felleman, Sara DeNobrega, Richie Kern, Kirsten Neuhaus, Heidi Gal, Collette Grecco, and Molly Gendell. And a huge thank you to Lynn Grady, Sean Newcott, Andrea Molitor, Ploy Siripant, Ben Steinberg, Kell Wilson, and Heidi Richter at Dey Street/HarperCollins.

To those who volunteered to share their stories, thank you. Some of the things you experienced were very personal, very intimate, and you didn't have to reveal anything. I am so grateful that you did.

And thank you to my "Peter," who was there during the most dynamic transition of my life so far—moving from secret, working-in-the-shadows exorcist to suddenly public exorcist. Those were intense, incredible, heartbreaking, profound years, but above all, it was pure magic. I will always love you for that.

And thank you, Spirit, for allowing me to do this, giving me what I now know is an extraordinary gift, and loving me through it all. I am forever grateful.

ABOUT THE AUTHOR

RACHEL STAVIS is a screenwriter for film, television, and video games. She has published four horror novels under the name R. H. Stavis. She is also an exorcist, doing her work pro bono and without advertising her services.